STUMP YOUR FRIENDS WITH FACTS AND STORIES ABOUT...

- The great team that never existed

- The batter who caught his own home run

- The hole-in-one that wasn't a hole-in-one

"Sports are the only entertainment where, no matter how many times you go, you never know the ending."

Neil Simon, American Playwright

Knowledge
in a Nutshell
ON SPORTS

arpr, inc.

Paperbacks

NOTE: To order additional copies of this book, please call the publisher, arpr, inc. 1-800-633-3082

Knowledge in a Nutshell on SPORTS is the second in the series of *Knowledge in a Nutshell books*

ISBN: 0-9660991-6-8

Printed in the United States of America by Geyer Printing Co. Pittsburgh, Pa.

arpr, inc. Paperbacks edition/November 1998

10 9 8 7 6 5 4 3 2 1

This book is dedicated to all of us who treasure the spirit, the participation, the teamwork, the enthusiasm and the enjoyment that sports brings to our lives.

These are the fun facts that happen in the field of sports every day.

TABLE OF CONTENTS

Preface

Each fact in this book has been carefully researched through at least three sources. We hope each fact and story will fascinate you, make you smile, wonder, think to yourself, "I didn't know that" or say to a friend, "I bet you didn't know..."

If we succeed in bringing a smile to your face when you share your new-found knowledge with someone else...then we will feel we have been successful in giving you some *Knowledge in a Nutshell on Sports.*

One

Football

Head coach skips game

There was a major-college game in which the head coach of one team—surprisingly—decided NOT to come to the game. In 1926, mighty Notre Dame had won 8 straight games, and their 9th opponent was little Carnegie Tech in Pittsburgh. Notre Dame coach Knute Rockne didn't think Carnegie Tech had much of a chance. He let his team be handled by assistants while he spent the day watching the Army-Navy game in Chicago. But Carnegie Tech shocked Notre Dame 19-0. It was called the biggest upset up to that time in football history, and it was Notre Dame's only loss that year.

College football's longest win streak

What's the record in college football for a team winning the most games in a row? The record is held by Oklahoma which won 47 straight games between 1953 and 1957. No other college team has ever equaled or topped that.

Great football team NEVER existed

In 1941, a group of Wall Street stockbrokers got together and invented a college football team which they named Plainfield Teachers College. They began calling newspapers each week, giving the score of Plainfield's imaginary games. Newspapers, assuming the scores were real, printed them each Sunday. As the season went on, the stockbrokers had Plainfield undefeated and unscored on, and they sent out feature stories about the team. Finally, the hoax was revealed and Plainfield went down in history as a great team that never was.

The last unscored-on team

What was the last college football team to go through an entire regular season and NOT allow ANY points to be scored against them all year? The last was Tennessee in 1939. Here's Tennessee's complete regular-season record that year. They beat North Carolina State 13-0, Sewanee 40-0, Chattanooga 28-0, Alabama 21-0, Mercer 17-0, LSU 20-0, Citadel 34-0, Vanderbilt 13-0, Kentucky 19-0, and Auburn 7-0.

The singular quiz

There are just 10 major-college football teams in the nation whose nicknames DON'T end in the letter "s". How many of the 10 can you name? They are the Alabama Crimson Tide; Illinois Illini; Marshall Thundering Herd; Navy Midshipmen; North Carolina State Wolfpack; Notre Dame Fighting Irish; Stanford Cardinal; Syracuse Orange; Tulane Green Wave; and the Tulsa Hurricane.

8-year-old girl names Super Bowl

When football owners were deciding what to call their championship game, Sharron Hunt, 8-year-old daughter of Lamar Hunt, who owns the Kansas City Chiefs, had been playing with the black rubber ball called a "super ball." From that she got the idea to suggest to her Dad that pro football name its title game the "Super Bowl." Lamar Hunt made that recommendation, and so the famous Super Bowl game really owes its name to a little girl.

The greatest performance

In the history of big-time football, no player ever had a day like Red Grange of Illinois had against Michigan on October 18, 1924. The first time he got the ball, he ran 95 yards for a touchdown. The second time he got the ball he ran 67 yards for a TD. The third time he got the ball he ran 56 yards for a TD. And the fourth time he got the ball he ran 44 yards for a touchdown. He had taken the ball 4 times, scored 4 times, covered 262 yards and still had not been stopped or tackled.

History books are wrong

Almost all football history books say the first college football game ever played was between Princeton and Rutgers on Nov. 6, 1869. But that's really not true. What they played that day wasn't football; it was soccer. There was NO running with the ball, NO passing and NO tackling. Football as we know it developed slowly over the years. Running with the ball, and tackling, came later in the 1800s, and passing didn't enter the game until the 1900s.

Greats never won Heisman

Surprisingly, most of the greatest quarterbacks in National Football League history NEVER won the Heisman Trophy in college football—including Joe Montana, Steve Young, Brett Favre, Dan Marino, Sammy Baugh, Johnny Unitas, Terry Bradshaw, Troy Aikman and John Elway.

NFL didn't have Super Bowl

The National Football League was in existence 46 years before the first Super Bowl game was played. The NFL started in 1920—but the first Super Bowl wasn't played until the end of the 1966 season.

Talk about a rout

What are the most points ever scored by one team in any college football game in history? The record was set by Georgia Tech. Georgia Tech beat Cumberland 222-0 in a game in 1916 to establish a record that's never been topped.

First Super Bowl coaches

Who were the head coaches in the first Super Bowl game? Vince Lombardi coached Green Bay to victory over Kansas City and their head coach, Hank Stram.

Oldest stadium

Of all the football stadiums in use in America today, the oldest is Harvard Stadium which was the first concrete football stadium built in the United States. It opened in 1903.

The one-armed football player

One of the most amazing football players of all time was Ellis Jones. Not only did he play major college football with one arm, but he won All-America recognition and played first-string on teams that went to 3 straight bowl games. Jones, who had lost his right arm in a childhood accident, was a starting guard for Tulsa University in 1942-43-44. With Jones as a starter, Tulsa won 23 games, lost only 2 and tied 1, and played in the Sugar Bowl twice and the Orange Bowl once.

One of history's biggest scientific discoveries born at football field

On Dec. 2, 1942, scientists, working under the stands at the University of Chicago's football stadium, created the first controlled nuclear chain reaction—and at that instant the atomic age was born. Chicago had given up football 3 years earlier, making their stadium available for the top-secret atomic experiments. And so, one of the biggest scientific milestones of all time occurred—of all places—in a football stadium.

Losing-team player wins Heisman

What player won the Heisman Trophy even though the team on which he played LOST 8 out of 10 games that season? Answer is Paul Hornung in 1956. That season Notre Dame won only two games and lost eight—but their quarterback, Paul Hornung, still won the Heisman.

A woman named John

Former coach Johnny Majors, who coached at Pitt, Iowa State and Tennessee, had a mother and father whose names were Shirley and John—except his father's name was Shirley and his mother's name was John. His father, Shirley Majors, was a long-time small-college coach. His mother was named John because that name was in the family tradition and when no boys came along in her generation, she inherited the name.

Harvard in a Rose Bowl?

Harvard was once chosen to play in the Rose Bowl game. Harvard played in the 1920 Rose Bowl, and won, beating Oregon 7-6.

High school game outdraws them all

The record for the biggest crowd ever to attend a football game was NOT set at a college or pro football game as you'd expect, but at a high school game. The all-time football attendance record was at Soldier Field, Chicago, Nov. 27, 1939, when 125,000 people came to see a high school playoff game with fabled Billy DeCorrovont.

Player scores 100 points in one game

No college football player ever matched this incredible record. In 1916, Leo Schlick of St. Viator College in Indiana scored 100 points against Lane College of Illinois. Schlick had 12 touchdowns and kicked 28 extra points in that game. His team won, 205-0.

Shula's surprising record

Although Don Shula was considered one of the great coaches in NFL history and won over 300 games, it may surprise you to learn that he never won a Super Bowl in the last 21 years of his coaching career. Shula won Super Bowls in 1973 and 1974—but then coached from 1975 through 1995 without ever winning a Super Bowl again.

Try this football riddle

You can predict the score of any football game before it even starts—AND BE RIGHT EVERY TIME. How can you do that? You can say—correctly—that the score of any game before it starts is always 0-0.

BOTH teams lost

Two Georgia high school football teams played each other in 1977 but after the game it was found that both used ineligible players. The Georgia High School Association then gave both teams a loss.

A priest writes famous football song

The Notre Dame "Victory March"—the song that starts out "Cheer, Cheer for Old Notre Dame," and is the best known football song of all time—was written by Father Michael Shea in 1909. One day, at a game that season, Father Shea decided Notre Dame should have an appropriate song. At the time, they didn't have one. After the game, Father Shea went to a nearby building, but someone was using the piano. So Father Shea then went to the Sacred Heart Church on campus and composed the song on the organ at the church. His brother, John Shea, then wrote the words. And so football's most famous fight song was written on a church organ.

New York? Giants and Jets

Two NFL teams NEVER play a home game in their home state. Both the New York Giants and New York Jets play their home games at Giants Stadium in East Rutherford, N.J.

Braves and Pirates played in NFL

Six of today's NFL teams had different nicknames when they started. The Washington Redskins original nickname was Braves. The New York Jets started as the Titans. The Chicago Bears first nickname was Staleys because they were sponsored by the Staley Starch Co. The Kansas City Chiefs franchise originally was in Dallas where the team's nickname was Texans. The Oilers are the Titans starting in 1999. And the Pittsburgh Steelers began in 1933 as the Pirates and didn't become known as the Steelers until 1940.

21 points in 35 seconds in NFL game

It happened in Pittsburgh Oct. 7, 1945. With 50 seconds to go in the first half, the New York Giants scored a TD. They kicked-off, Pittsburgh fumbled, the Giants recovered, and on the first play Arnie Herber threw a TD pass. On the next kickoff, Pittsburgh fumbled again, Bill Piccollo of New York scooped up the ball, and ran for a TD. There were 15 seconds to go. That was 21 points (all extra points were good) in just 35 seconds.

Only one bowl game?

Although there are many post-season football bowl games these days, it took football promoters a long time to catch on to the idea. The first Rose Bowl game was played in 1902 and, oddly enough, it was then more than 30 years later until other bowls such as the Orange, Sugar and Cotton started.

Madden tops Lombardi

Surprisingly, John Madden, now the TV football announcer, but formerly coach of the Raiders in the NFL, won a higher percentage of games than the legendary Vince Lombardi. Here are their career records as head coaches in regular season games in the National Football League: Lombardi won 96 games, lost 34 and tied 6 for a percentage of .728; Madden won 103, lost 32 and tied 7 for a percentage of .750.

The most unusual road trip

Willamette University of Salem, Ore., traveled to the University of Hawaii for a football game on Dec. 6, 1941. But the Japanese bombing of Pearl Harbor happened the next morning—and the team was stranded on the island. Most of the team finally returned to Oregon in early 1942, serving as aides on a hospital ship. But some of the players didn't conclude their road trip UNTIL 1945, since they immediately enlisted in the military and were shipped to the South Pacific to fight in the war.

The amazing Stanford-Cal game

Some experts say the most incredible play in college football history was in the Stanford-California game of 1982. It was California's 5-lateral, 57-yard kickoff return as time ran out when Cal players had to dodge not only all the Stanford players—but also the Stanford band that had rushed onto the field prematurely. The last Cal player crashed into a trombone player as he went into the end zone for the winning touchdown.

He saw a few football games

Here's one record that probably will never be broken. Amos Alonzo Stagg was a football coach for 70—that's right—70 consecutive years. He started out as coach at Springfield in 1890 and 1891. Then he coached at the University of Chicago from 1892 through 1932. He was at College of Pacific from 1933 through 1946, at Susquehanna from 1947 through 1952 and at Stockton from 1953 to 1960.

One All-America designation wasn't enough for him

Here's the story of one of the most amazing football players of all time. This man was so outstanding that he became the only player in football history ever named All-America at 2 different positions the same year. His name: Bronko Nagurski. He played fullback on offense and tackle on defense for the University of Minnesota in 1929 and was selected All-America at BOTH positions.

They won by losing

In 1942, Boston College was the number one team in the country. They were undefeated going into the last game with Holy Cross. They were heavily favored, and made reservations to hold a victory celebration after the game at a place called the Coconut Grove. However, in one of the greatest upsets in football history, Holy Cross not only beat BC, but they beat them by the score of 55-12. The crushed Boston College officials cancelled the "Victory" party. That night, the Coconut Grove caught fire. It was one of the worst disasters in history with 492 people losing their lives. The Boston College football players all might have been killed—except for the fact that they lost a football game that afternoon.

Woman coaches college football team

Yale's famous coach Walter Camp was ill during part of the 1892 season, and was unable to attend practices or games. His wife, Alice, went to the practices and games for him, and in effect, coached the football team that year. Yale went undefeated.

Why are they the Packers?

How did the Green Bay Packers get that nickname? They were originally financed by the Acme Packing Company of Green Bay, and since employees of the company were called "packers," they chose "Packers" as the team's name.

Owner does unusual thing to get a player

The first great NFL passer was Benny Friedman of Detroit. In 1929, the owner of the New York Giants BOUGHT THE WHOLE DETROIT TEAM just to get Friedman. The Detroit team went out of business and Friedman played in New York. The city of Detroit was then without an NFL team until a new Detroit franchise arrived 6 years later.

Who has the ball?

For the first 60 years or so of football, up to the 1930s, spectators at games had real trouble knowing what was going on. Until the 1930s, most players didn't wear numbers and most stadiums didn't have public address systems. A lot of people didn't know who carried the ball or who made a tackle.

Why "Crimson Tide"?

The Alabama-Auburn football game of 1907 was played on a muddy field and a reporter wrote that Alabama, wearing red jerseys, moved through the mud like a "crimson tide." That stuck and became the official nickname of the team.

MVP a loser

It's hard to believe a player on the losing team in the Super Bowl would be voted the Most Valuable Player for that game—but that's what happened in 1971. The Most Valuable Player in that game was linebacker Chuck Howley of Dallas. He was voted MVP of the Super Bowl even though his team lost.

Rechichar's amazing first kick

Before Sept. 27, 1953, Bert Rechichar of the Baltimore Colts had never been called on to kick a field goal in the NFL. But on that date, Rechichar was told to try a long 56-yard field goal. Up to that time nobody in NFL history had ever kicked one that far. Rechichar's kick was good—and, thus, he set an all-time NFL record on his first attempt. In another amazing fact, Rechichar played 8 years after that and never kicked one that long again.

Smallest school to play big-time football

Little St. Mary's College of Moraga, Calif., once competed in major-college football with a student body of only about 150. Despite that small size, they had a combined record of 13-3 in 1945 and 1946, playing such teams as UCLA, California and Southern Cal. And, little St. Mary's played in the Sugar Bowl on New Year's Day, 1946, against Oklahoma State.

The famous "Heidi Game"

Here's how that game got its name. The New York Jets were playing the Oakland Raiders in 1968. NBC was televising the game nationally and ended the telecast with 2 minutes remaining so they could air, on time, at 7 p.m. Eastern time, the children's classic movie, "Heidi." The Jets were leading 32-29, but then the Raiders scored 2 touchdowns in those last 2 minutes, and came from behind to win 43-32. TV viewers never saw that rally. There was a huge public outcry—and the game went into football lore as the "Heidi" game.

Bear was right again

Legendary Alabama football coach Bear Bryant once said that when he stopped coaching he would die. Following the 1982 season, after beating Illinois in the Liberty Bowl, Bryant gave up his coaching job and retired. LESS THAN ONE MONTH LATER, on Jan. 26, 1983, Bryant died.

The legendary Vow Boys

The freshmen football players at Stanford in 1932 vowed that when they became sophomores, juniors and seniors, they would win the conference title and go to the Rose Bowl each year. They were nicknamed the "Vow Boys"—and they kept their vow. The Stanford teams of 1933, '34 and '35 did indeed win the right to play in the Rose Bowl game those 3 straight years.

Why is it a touchdown?

One of the strangest words in sports is "touchdown" in football. There's NO rule requiring a player to touch the ball to the ground when he scores a "touchdown."

Monday Night football pioneers

Who were the announcers when Monday Night Football started on national TV in 1970? The original Monday Night announcing crew was Howard Cosell, Don Meredith and Keith Jackson.

Women's college now a football power

A former all-women's college is now a national power in men's major-college football. It's a little-remembered fact that Florida State University was an all-women's college from 1901 until 1947 when they admitted men for the first time.

Football

Who would have predicted success for Seifert?

Here's an oddity about the man who was one of the most successful coaches in NFL history—George Seifert. Seifert won two Super Bowls and had a top winning percentage with the 49ers, but just the opposite was true when he was a college head coach. He won only 6 games—and lost 18. Seifert coached one year at Westminster College in Utah where he was 3-3, then coached 2 years at Cornell where he won 3 and lost 15.

One game—two fields

There was a football game in 1988 that was played on 2 different fields—on the same day. The game was between Troy (Ala.) State and visiting Southeast Missouri State. It started in Troy's Memorial Stadium—but the lights in the stadium failed early in the 4th quarter. School officials decided to continue the game at a lighted practice field a third of a mile away. It's believed that's the only college game in history that started on one field and finished on another the same day.

Paul Brown showed them

The Cleveland Browns of 1950 were ridiculed by some NFL teams for passing too much, so Cleveland coach Paul Brown decided to show the world he could win without passing at all. In a game on Dec. 3, 1950 against Philadelphia, with first place at stake, the Browns played the whole game without ever throwing a pass—and they won 13-7. There's never been an NFL game since then when a team went through an entire game without throwing a pass.

Gloomy Frank Leahy

Many football coaches make pessimistic statements, in hopes of keeping their team from being over-confident, but the extreme pessimist of all time was probably Frank Leahy, who coached Notre Dame in the 1940s and '50s. Leahy once said, "I honestly feel we won't make a first down this year." (Notre Dame went undefeated that year.)

Summerall's invisible field goal

One of the most unusual field goals ever kicked was by the now-TV announcer, Pat Summerall. His strange kick decided a key game in 1958. The New York Giants and Cleveland were tied 10-10 with seconds left. Summerall of the Giants tried a field goal from the 42-yard line in a swirling snowstorm. The ball went up in the air and was completely LOST FROM VIEW IN THE SNOW. Nobody could see the ball. Then, all of a sudden, it reappeared, dropped down over the goal post, and gave the Giants the win and a playoff berth.

Small cheering section

You probably won't believe this one, but it's true. There was once a major-college football game that had a paid attendance of one. It was the Washington State-San Jose game of Nov. 12, 1955 played at Washington State. The temperature that day was 14 below zero and only one person showed up to pay his way into the stadium.

The Steagles and Card-Pitts

Strange things happened in the NFL in the 1940s. In 1943, the Pittsburgh Steelers merged with the Eagles and played under the name of "Steagles." Despite having two rosters to choose from, they finished next to last in their division. The next year, Pittsburgh merged with the Cardinals and were known as the "Card-Pitts." Again, despite having two rosters from which to staff their team, they lost every game they played.

Little school in big bowl game

What was the smallest school ever to play in the Rose Bowl game? Little Washington and Jefferson College of Washington, Pa., played in the Rose Bowl game of 1922. W&J which had just about 400 students, tied California in that Rose Bowl, 0-0.

"Outlined against a blue, gray October sky…"

What has been called the most famous newspaper story in sports was Grantland Rice's report when he covered the Army-Notre Dame football game on Oct. 18, 1924 and coined the nickname for football's great backfield, the Four Horsemen. Rice wrote, "Outlined against a blue, gray October sky, the Four Horsemen rode again. In dramatic lore they are known as famine, pestilence, destruction and death. These are only aliases. Their real names are Stuhldreher, Miller, Crowley and Layden. They formed the crest of the South Bend cyclone…as Notre Dame beat Army." The Four Horsemen played together 3 seasons, winning 27 games and losing to only one team—Nebraska.

4 U.S. Presidents played college football

Dwight Eisenhower was a halfback at Army in 1912; Richard Nixon, a lineman at Whittier College in 1931-32-33; Gerald Ford, a center at Michigan in 1932-33-34; and Ronald Reagan, a halfback at Eureka College in 1930-31.

Hold that tackle

Surprisingly, at one time in the National Football League, ball carriers could get up and keep running AFTER they were tackled. Plays ended only when runners were held down. If they weren't held down, they could run for more yards. That rule wasn't changed until 1955.

How wide is a football field?

Oddly enough, here's a football question that looks easy, but it's surprising how few fans—even the really good ones—can answer it. The question: Everybody knows a football field is 100 yards long from goal line to goal line—but, how WIDE is a football field? A football field is 160 feet or 53 and one-third yards wide.

Notre Dame wasn't the Fighting Irish

Although one of the most famous nicknames in sports is Notre Dame's—the "Fighting Irish"—Notre Dame originally did NOT have that nickname. They didn't adopt "Fighting Irish" for their teams until 1927. From the 1880s through 1926, Notre Dame's nicknames were "Hoosiers" and "Ramblers."

Sunday games illegal

The Pittsburgh Steelers and Philadelphia Eagles could not join the NFL during the league's early years for a very good reason. The NFL requires its teams to play most of its games on Sundays—but the state of Pennsylvania had a law prohibiting Sunday games (and movies, too) until 1933. Only when that law was repealed in a close vote were the Eagles and Steelers able to join the NFL.

He didn't know what is was like to lose

There was a college coach who NEVER lost a game in his first ELEVEN YEARS as a coach. Gil Dobie's amazing streak started at North Dakota State in 1906 and 1907 where he had 2 undefeated teams and continued at the University of Washington from 1908 through 1916 where his record was 58-0 with 3 ties. After 11 years of coaching, Dobie finally found out what it was like to lose when he lost a game in 1917—twelve years after he started.

The first Heisman winner's amazing run

The most spectacular run in football, according to some experts, was made by the man who won the first Heisman Trophy, Jay Berwanger. In a game against Ohio State, Berwanger had an 85-yard touchdown run in which he zig-zagged down the field breaking 11 tackles on the play. Every one of his 11 opponents tried, and failed, to tackle him. He went into and out of the grasp of EVERY opponent on the field.

NFL didn't like Super Bowl

Although the National Football League now proudly uses the words "Super Bowl" to describe its title game each year, the NFL used a different official name for the game until the 5th Super Bowl. Up to that time, people in the NFL didn't like the name "Super Bowl," and used the term "AFC-NFC World Championship Game" instead. The 5th Super Bowl, played in 1971, was the first to be officially called the "Super Bowl."

Smartest Team?

One of the most unusual football teams of all time was Dartmouth's in 1925. They won the national championship that year with an undefeated team—and there were 22 Phi Beta Kappas on the squad. There never has been another team in history like Dartmouth of 1925.

A top college named itself after its football coach

Sam Colgate was football coach of Madison College in Hamilton, N.Y. in the 1890s. Coach Colgate and his family made a large donation to the college and the name of the school was changed from Madison to Colgate. So, today, Colgate University is named after its former football coach.

Would this happen today?

A major-college football coach once insisted that officials TAKE AWAY a touchdown from his team because he noticed a penalty that the officials missed. It happened when the legendary Amos Alonzo Stagg was coaching. Stagg was so strict, he wouldn't accept a touchdown his team scored when he knew they had committed a penalty on that play.

Why are they called "bowl" games?

The phrase "bowl game" came into our language in 1923 when Pasadena's originally-named Tournament of Roses game moved to a newly-built, circular, bowl-shaped stadium. A California publicity man named both the stadium and the game the "Rose Bowl." After that, other post-season games called themselves "bowl games," even though many of them—oddly enough—aren't played in circular bowl-like stadiums.

Why 11 players?

Ever wonder why football is played with 11 players on each side—and not some other number? When the first football game was played in America between Princeton and Rutgers in 1869, there were 25 on each side. The size of teams varied until 1880 when Yale's Walter Camp standardized the rules. He decided on 11 players per side because he was influenced by soccer and cricket, both of which happen to have 11 players per team. And that's why American football has 11 players.

The Ivy Leaguers were most powerful

It's hard to believe now, but teams from the Ivy League used to win the national championship in major-college football often. In the first 50 years of American football, Ivy League teams from Yale, Harvard, Princeton, Penn and Cornell won the national football championship more than 30 times.

Hold all bets

There was a college football game in which the score—and even the winner—were changed 48 hours after the game was over. It happened in 1940. Cornell beat Dartmouth 7-3. But on the Monday after that Saturday game, officials of both schools looked at films of the game and realized Cornell had scored its touchdown on an illegal 5th down play. Even though Cornell had an unbeaten season going, they said they'd give up the touchdown, and thereby give up the victory. The result was declared reversed and it was officially changed in the record books from Cornell 7, Dartmouth 3 to Dartmouth 3, Cornell 0.

Best runner in NFL?

Although there have been lots of great runners in the NFL, nobody has ever come close to the record set many years ago by Beattie Feathers. Feathers, a rookie from the University of Tennessee, joined the Chicago Bears in 1934. He carried the ball 101 times rushing that season and gained 1,004 yards, which means he averaged almost 10 yards every time he took the ball from scrimmage. That record by Feathers has lasted in the NFL for over 60 years—and it looks as if nobody will ever break it. At least, nobody has in all the years since Feathers set it.

One-eyed wonder

A man once became a star quarterback in the NFL even though he was blind in one eye—and often couldn't see part of the field when he went back to pass. Tommy Thompson quarterbacked the Philadelphia Eagles to the NFL championship in 1948 and 1949, and led the league in passing statistics in 1948 even though he was blind in his left eye.

Young coach wins big

Who was the youngest head coach ever to win the national championship in major-college football? Answer is Danny Ford whose Clemson Tigers won the national title in 1981 when Ford was 33 years old.

Shakespeare lives

William Shakespeare was a first-round draft pick in the NFL. The Pittsburgh Steelers drafted William Shakespeare No. 1 in the 1936 draft. This William Shakespeare was a star quarterback from Notre Dame.

Where was the offense?

Has any college football team ever gone through a whole season and not scored ANY points ALL YEAR? It happened 3 times in the 20th century. The 3 teams that failed to score any points in any game throughout an entire season were Villanova in 1923, Carnegie Tech in 1946 and St. Paul's College in 1952.

Notre Dame turns green

One of the great psychological moves by a football coach was pulled off by Knute Rockne at Notre Dame in 1927. His team was playing Navy. The Notre Dame players were, as usual, wearing their blue jerseys at the start of the game. But after Navy scored in the first quarter, the Notre Dame players all pulled off their blue jerseys and then played in the green jerseys they had been wearing underneath. That surprising move seemed to change the momentum of the game. In their new green jerseys, Notre Dame took command of the game and won 19-6.

The nothing series

One of the most unbelievable football series of all time was between the University of Pittsburgh and Fordham University. They played 3 games, in 1935, '36 and '37 and, amazingly, NEITHER team scored ANY points in ANY OF THOSE GAMES. They played 3 straight 0-0 games.

Who needs a coach?

Yale played 12 football seasons from 1876 through 1887 without a coach and won 71 games while losing only 2—and that's the best 12-year record in the history of the school—better than in all the years they've had coaches. In those days, the playing captains ran the team at Yale.

NFL team goes to the dogs

The National Football League once had a team named after a dog kennel. There was a team in 1922 and '23 that went by the name of "Oorang"— and if you look at the NFL standings for those years, you'll see Oorang won 2 games in 1922 and 1 game in '23. Oorang played out of Marion, Ohio and was named after the Oorang Dog Kennels of Marion, who owned the team.

How can you run 5 yards and score 4 touchdowns?

This oddity happened on Nov. 4, 1973, when Bobby Douglass of the Chicago Bears ran just 5 yards and yet scored 4 TDs. His first carry was a 2-yard touchdown run, and the other 3 were each 1-yard TD runs. Douglass' total yardage gained rushing was 5 yards, but he had scored 4 touchdowns.

Double Heisman winner

Who's the only man to win the Heisman Trophy in 2 different years? The answer: Archie Griffin of Ohio State who won it in both 1974 and 1975.

He scored all the points for both teams

Byron Haines of Washington, in a 1935 game against Southern Cal, scored a touchdown for his own team, and later in the game was tackled behind his own goal line, giving a safety to his opponents. The final score of the contest was 6-2, so Haines scored all the points.

The owner plays

Can you imagine the owner of an NFL team putting on a uniform, going out on the field, and being a regular player on his own team? George Halas did it for 10 years. Halas owned the Chicago Bears and from 1920 through 1929, he was an end on the team. As an owner-player, Halas set an NFL record that lasted 49 years when he ran 98 yards for a touchdown in a 1923 game.

How Duke's famous unscored-on season ended

Duke was undefeated AND unscored-on throughout the 1938 season, and then met Southern Cal in the Rose Bowl. Duke led 3-0 with 41 seconds to go. But Southern Cal's 4th-string quarterback, Doyle Nave, then threw a touchdown pass to win 7-3. Duke had held all opponents scoreless for 599-minutes and 19-seconds in their 600-minute season, but lost their unbeaten and unscored-on record with just 41 seconds remaining in one of the great games of all time.

TD's worth nothing

In the early days of football, touchdowns counted for nothing. In those days, a touchdown merely gave a team the right to "convert" the touchdown into a score by kicking the ball over the goal posts. This feature is still retained in today's point-after-touchdown conversion.

The Salad Bowl

There used to be a football bowl game called the Salad Bowl. It was played every New Year's Day from 1948 through 1952 in Phoenix. The last Salad Bowl, played Jan. 1, 1952, saw Houston beat Dayton 26-21.

30,000 empty seats for Super Bowl

The first Super Bowl, played in 1967, failed to sell out by a big margin. The game was played in the 93,000-seat Los Angeles Coliseum. The attendance was 63,000.

Winningest coaches

Of all major college coaches in history, which one won the greatest percentage of games over a career? The answer is Knute Rockne of Notre Dame who won 88% of all the games he coached (105 wins, 12 losses). Ranking second in history is Frank Leahy, who coached at both Notre Dame and Boston College. Leahy won 86% of his games (107 wins, 13 losses).

Biggest upset

The biggest upset in football history, based on the predicted point-spread, was the NFL title game on Dec. 8, 1940 between the Chicago Bears and the Washington Redskins. The Redskins were favored by 7 points. But the Bears won, 73-0, making an 80-point difference from the predicted margin to the actual one—and that's the biggest error the odds-makers have ever made.

First woman to play in college football game

Liz Heaston made history. Heaston, a soccer player at Willamette (Ore.) College, played in Willamette's football game against Linfield College, on Oct. 18, 1997. She kicked 2 extra points in Willamette's 27-0 win.

What a start

One of the most unusual seasons any football team ever had was the one the Chicago Bears experienced in 1932. The Bears opened that season by playing three straight 0-0 games. They lost their next game 2-0. Thus, after 4 games, they hadn't even scored a point—but they wound up the season in first place and won the championship. They finished with the odd record of 7 wins, 1 loss and 6 ties, and that turned out to be the best record in the National Football League that year.

They didn't run, they didn't pass—but they won

There was a college football game in which one team did not run or pass the ball at ANY time during the entire game, and still won it. In a game in the early 1900s, Kentucky decided to punt on first down every time they got the ball. They never ran the ball and never passed. And they won 12-6 by recovering two fumbles by their opponents in the end zone. This oddity is hard to believe but it's been verified by the Kentucky Athletic Department.

Road games didn't bother Irish

Notre Dame set an amazing football record when they won every game one season—even though they never played a home game that year. It happened in 1929. The new Notre Dame Stadium was being built while the old one had already been dismantled, forcing the Irish to play all games on the road. Yet they went undefeated—the ONLY unbeaten team in history that played all games away from home.

They could have sold 1 million tickets

Which football game in history had the biggest request for tickets? It was a game in the days before national TV, in 1946, between unbeaten Army and unbeaten Notre Dame. More than 1-million ticket requests were received. The game featured 3 of the top 4 Heisman Trophy finalists that year—Doc Blanchard and Glenn Davis of Army, and Johnny Lujack of Notre Dame. But the game was somewhat of a dud. The final score was 0-0.

Father to son

What man replaced his father as head coach of an NFL team? The answer is Wade Phillips who became head coach of the New Orleans Saints during the 1985 season, replacing his father, Bum Phillips, who resigned. Wade had been an assistant coach with the team.

The first cheerleaders

How did the custom of cheerleaders start in football? When the first intercollegiate game was played in 1869 between Princeton and Rutgers, Princeton players got the idea of trying to upset Rutgers players by yelling every time Rutgers put the ball in play. But there was one thing wrong with this plan. Although the yelling did upset Rutgers, at the same time, it bothered the Princeton players because they had to use too much effort in yelling and it distracted them from their own play. So, for the second game against Rutgers, a Princeton man got the great idea of putting some of the students along the sideline to lead the yelling instead of the players. A few students were chosen and taught what to yell and when to yell. And that's how the tradition was born.

NFL no big deal

The first year the NFL published attendance figures was in 1934 and the average attendance that season was 8,211 per game.

Harvard wins 29-29

One of the most amazing comebacks ever seen in football happened in a game between Yale and Harvard in 1968. Yale led 29-13 with only 43 seconds left. But Harvard scored two touchdowns and a pair of two-point conversions in just 42 seconds to finish the game tied 29-29. The Harvard newspaper used the famous headline: HARVARD BEATS YALE, 29-29.

Quarterbacks didn't pass

Until the 1940s, the passer on most football teams was NOT the quarterback. Before the T-formation became popular, the passing was almost always done by a halfback. In fact quarterbacks seldom handled the ball. In the single wing formations used by most teams, quarterbacks were used only as blockers.

This coach was busy

Believe it or not, a man was once head coach of a college football team AND an NFL team at the SAME TIME.   Buff Donelli was head coach of the Pittsburgh Steelers of the NFL and of Duquesne University in Pittsburgh in 1941—running practice for one in the morning and the other in the afternoon. Finally, the NFL ordered Donelli to choose one job or the other, and he gave up the Steeler post; but not before making football history for part of the 1941 season.

A different kind of football explosion

A football once exploded during a game— and caused a team to lose. It happened in the 1929 Rose Bowl. Benny Lom of California punted from his own 9-yard line but his kick punctured the ball. All the air came out, and the ball collapsed right on the 9. Georgia Tech took over there and scored the winning touchdown.

A strange way to score a TD

There was once a football game when a PLAYER—and not a pass—was thrown for a touchdown. Tennessee lined up for a play on the Alabama 1-yard line. Running back Sam McAllester got the ball and several of his teammates then picked him up and threw him across the goal line for a touchdown. That happened in the early years of football and soon after that, rules were changed to prohibit that play. But throwing a player for a TD enabled Tennessee to win 7-0.

Talk about a raw rookie

A man once played in an NFL game even though he had never seen a game in his life until he took the field that day. Garo Yepremian, a soccer player from Cyprus, was visiting the U.S. when he was urged to try out with the Detroit Lions during the season. He was hired on the spot and kicked off that week in the Lions game against Baltimore on Oct. 16, 1966—playing in the first American football game he ever saw.

Why is it named the Heisman trophy?

The trophy was named after a man who happened to be the athletic director of the Downtown Athletic Club of New York, retired coach, John Heisman. The Downtown Athletic Club came up with the idea for the trophy and named it after him.

Football team wears pink uniforms

When Syracuse University fielded its first football team, in 1889, the school color was pink and the players wore pink uniforms. The team had a terrible year. Those pink uniforms lasted just one season. The next year, Syracuse changed their school color, uniforms and nickname to orange—and they've been known as the Orangemen ever since.

Win one for the Gipper

One of football's great legends concerns George Gipp, who played his last season for Notre Dame in 1920. Here are the details of that legend. Gipp became ill during his senior year and was on his deathbed. Coach Knute Rockne came to visit, and Gipp gave Rockne the basis for the most famous pep talk in football history. Gipp reportedly said, "I've got to go now, Rock. It's all right. But sometime, Rock, when the team's up against it; when things are wrong and the breaks are beating the boys, tell them to go in there with all they've got—and win one for the Gipper." Rockne waited until halftime of the Notre Dame-Army game of 1928. He used Gipp's last words as his pep talk. Needless to say, Notre Dame won that day.

How good a player was George Gipp?

Oddly enough, George Gipp never played high school football, and didn't even go out for football when he first came to Notre Dame. But Coach Knute Rockne saw Gipp fooling around with a football one day and urged him to join the team. Gipp went on to become one of the great all-around players in football history. He could kick, run and pass. He set records from 1918 to 1920 that lasted for years. Gipp died of strep throat 2 weeks after the last game of the season—and became a legendary inspiration.

Two

Baseball

Even Mark McGwire didn't do this

The most incredible home-run hitting by one player in one pro baseball game was in the Texas League in 1902 when Jay Clarke of Corsicana hit 8 HOMERS HIMSELF IN 9 INNINGS. Nobody has come close to that record in pro baseball history. But oddly enough, when Clarke got to the majors, he hit only 6 homers in 9 YEARS.

They'll never retire Cobb's number

Baseball CAN'T retire the uniform number of one of the greatest players in history, Hall-of-Famer Ty Cobb. The reason is that Cobb wore NO number on his uniform. All baseball teams didn't start using uniform numbers until 1929—and Cobb retired in 1928. He never had a number.

How can you catch your own home run?

A big league baseball player once caught his own home run. It happened to Dixie Walker one day in 1946 at Ebbets Field, Brooklyn. Walker hit a homer with the ball sticking, then staying, in the right field screen high above the field. At the end of the inning, Walker went out to play his position in right field, and as he neared the fence the ball suddenly started to drop out of the screen. Walker ran over, made the catch, and became the only man in history who ever caught his own home run.

The fans called the plays

Master showman Bill Veeck who owned the old St. Louis Browns of baseball's American League came up with the idea. On Aug. 24, 1951, he gave posters reading "YES" and "NO" to the fans and allowed them to vote on what the Browns should do at various points in the game. It worked. St. Louis won, 5-3.

Try this baseball riddle

How can a team get 3 triples and 3 singles in one inning, and still NOT score a run? Answer: First 2 players triple and are out at the plate trying for an inside-the-park homer. Next player triples and stays at third. Next 2 players get infield singles with the runner holding third. Last player smacks a ground ball that hits the runner going from first to second. The batter gets credit for a hit, but the runner is out, making 3 triples, 3 singles, 3 outs...and no runs.

This player literally ran through a wall

Rightfielder Rodney McCray of the Pacific Coast League was chasing a fly ball in a 1991 game. He just kept running—and ran right THROUGH the plywood fence at Civic Stadium in Portland, Ore. McCray didn't catch the ball, but he wasn't seriously hurt, suffering a bloody nose and a bump on his head—and he became a TV highlight star.

He hits 3 homers into 3 states—in the SAME game

Olympic champion Jim Thorpe played in a semi-pro baseball game in a ballpark on the Texas-Oklahoma-Arkansas border. He hit his first homer over the leftfield wall with the ball landing in Oklahoma. Then he hit a homer over the rightfield wall, into Arkansas. His third homer of the game was an inside-the-park home run in centerfield, which was in Texas.

Who was the greatest player of all time?

How about Babe Ruth—because not only was Ruth a great hitter, but unknown to many, he was also a great pitcher. Before Ruth became famous for his home runs and high lifetime batting average, he spent the early years of his big league career as a top pitcher, winning over 90 games and leading the league in earned run average.

The missing man in the Hall of Fame

Although baseball's Hall of Fame is in Cooperstown, N.Y., because that was the hometown of baseball's supposed inventor, Abner Doubleday—oddly enough, Doubleday himself is NOT in the Hall of Fame. Most voters over the years have doubted that Doubleday really invented baseball, so they've kept him out EVEN THOUGH IT WAS BUILT THERE IN THE FIRST PLACE BECAUSE OF HIM.

Why the Dodgers are the Dodgers

One of the most unusual nicknames for any team in the big leagues is the Dodgers and here's how it happened. The name was first applied to the Dodgers when they were in Brooklyn, years before they moved to Los Angeles. When trolleys were introduced in Brooklyn, people there were called "trolley dodgers" because so many trolleys rumbled down their streets. The Brooklyn baseball team was then named the "Trolley Dodgers." After a while, they shortened it to simply "Dodgers."

Pitcher wins 20 games TWICE in ONE season

Jack Chesbro of the 1904 New York Yankees won 20 games by July and then won 21 more before the end of the season for a total of 41 victories. Chesbro won 41 and lost 12 that year.

Forget home runs

There was once a big league park where it was ALMOST IMPOSSIBLE TO HIT A HOME RUN OVER THE FENCE. It was Braves Field in Boston, which was in use from 1915 until the Braves moved out of Boston in 1953. NOBODY hit a homer over the fence there the first two years the park was used. And in 6 years, only 2 homers were hit. It was over 400 feet down each foul line and over 550 feet to center field—making it the biggest ballpark in playing area in major league history. The distances were later shortened, but for some years, Braves Field was the all-time pitcher's paradise.

What-might-have-been for Tony

Tony Conigliaro might well have become the greatest home run hitter of all time—surpassing Hank Aaron and Babe Ruth. It's a little-remembered fact that Conigliaro hit 104 homers in the majors by the time he was 22 years old, and by comparison, Aaron had hit only 66 homers by age 22—and Ruth had hit only 9. But then on Aug. 19, 1967, at age 22, Conigliaro was hit in the face by a pitch and suffered an eye injury that curtailed his career. Had Conigliaro not suffered that injury, he might have become the top home run hitter of all time, considering the start he had.

The owner also manages

Who was the last owner of a big league baseball team to also serve as manager of that team? Answer is Ted Turner. Turner took over as manager of the Atlanta Braves for one game in the 1977 season.

Aaron first in more ways than one

If you arrange the names of all the thousands of men who've ever played big league baseball in alphabetical order, the name that comes first is Hank Aaron. Isn't it odd that the man who stands first on the all-time home run list should also stand first on the all-time alphabetical list of all the major leaguers in history?

Why not batball?

Baseball almost had a different name. Some early players called the game "batball"—and when you think about it, "batball" is just as logical a name for the game as "baseball," since bats are used just as much as bases.

Ryan faced dads and sons

Nolan Ryan pitched in big league baseball so long—a record 27 years—he struck out 6 father-and-son combinations. He struck out Bobby Bonds and Bobby's son, Barry; Maury and Bump Wills; Sandy Alomar and Sandy Jr.; Ken Griffey and Ken Jr.; Dick Schofield and Dick Jr.; and Tito and Terry Francona.

Manager doesn't know baseball

A man once became the manager of a big league baseball team even though he really didn't know much about baseball. Judge Emil Fuchs inherited the ownership of the Braves in 1929 and astounded everyone by deciding to become the manager. Judge Fuchs lasted one season, and the Braves finished last.

The magic of 90 feet

An amazing fact of pro baseball is that when the first rules were made over 100 years ago, the distance between the bases was arbitrarily set at 90 feet, a distance that's never been changed. Sportswriter Red Smith once wrote, "The world's fastest man can't run to first base ahead of a sharply hit ball that is cleanly handled by an infielder; yet let the fielder juggle the ball for just an instant and the runner will be safe. Ninety feet also accurately measures the speed of a base-stealer against the speed of a thrown ball. Ninety feet demands perfection—and nobody knows for sure how it came to be." Although today's players are bigger and faster, 90 feet between the bases works as well now as it did 100 years ago.

The pitcher who lost the most games

Cy Young won more games than any pitcher in big league history –511—but who holds the record for losing the most games of all time in the majors? Answer is that same Cy Young. He lost 315 games, and no one else is close to that record.

Hard-luck Harvey

The man who hurled THE best-pitched game in big league history, incredibly, wound up losing that game. On May 26, 1959, Harvey Haddix pitched a perfect game for 12 innings, the only time in the majors anybody ever did that. He retired 36 consecutive batters, an all-time record for one game—but his own team didn't score and he lost the game in the 13th inning. Thus the greatest-ever pitching performance resulted in a loss.

Who needs .300 hitters

A big league team once won the pennant without having any .300 hitters in their regular lineup. The Los Angeles Dodgers won the 1965 pennant without a .300 hitter. Among all the Dodger regulars, the man who had the highest average that season was Maury Wills who batted .286.

Surprising home run record

Which big league player led the league in home runs the most consecutive years? The answer is NOT Babe Ruth or Hank Aaron as you might expect. It's Ralph Kiner, who led the National League in homers for 7 consecutive seasons from 1946 through 1952. The most consecutive years Ruth won the home run championship were 6, and the most years in a row Aaron did it were 2.

Most homers, all time

It's easy to guess which 3 players have hit the most home runs in major league baseball history—Hank Aaron, Babe Ruth and Willie Mays—but who ranks No. 4 and No. 5? The man who hit the 4th most homers in history is Frank Robinson, and No. 5 on the all-time list is Harmon Killebrew.

His one complete game was a beaut

Bobo Holloman pitched only one complete big league game in his life—but that one game was a no-hitter. Despite pitching a no-hitter in the American League in 1953, Holloman was never able to pitch any other complete game in the majors before that or after that.

Why the Best Pitcher Award is the "Cy" Young Award

One of the great pitchers in baseball history was Cy Young—but his real name was Denton Young. His fastball was described as being as fast as a cyclone—and that's how he got the nickname Cy.

Baseball

No Gold Glove for Jolley

A big league outfielder once made THREE errors on one play. Smead Jolley was playing the outfield for the White Sox in 1930. The batter hit a single and the ball rolled through Jolley's legs for error number one. Jolley turned to get the rebound off the wall but the ball went back through his legs again, for error number two. Then he finally got hold of the ball, but he threw it wild—into the stands—for his third error on the same play.

What an arm

One of the most amazing records in sports is one set by Glenn Gorbous, an outfielder for the Phillies in 1957. He set a world record by throwing a baseball, officially 444 feet, or 148 yards—and that's incredible when you consider he threw a ball—in the air—the length of a football field PLUS 48 more yards.

Fidel in the majors?

Several major league baseball teams once scouted Cuban dictator Fidel Castro when he was a promising young pitcher in Cuba years ago. World history might have been changed if one of those teams had signed Castro and he had become a pitcher in the U.S., instead of staying home and turning to politics.

Why are they Pirates?

How did Pittsburgh's big league baseball team get the name Pirates? In 1890, Pittsburgh signed some players who were already under contract to another team. Because of their actions the league dubbed them "Pirates," and the name has remained.

No long game here

Believe it or not, a complete 9-inning big league baseball game was once played in 51 minutes. It was a game between the Giants and Phils in 1919.

Shoeless Joe had no luck

Shoeless Joe Jackson had American League season batting averages of .387, .408, .395, .373, .354 and .382—AND NEVER WON A BATTING TITLE. Every year, starting in 1910, when he had such high averages, someone else had a better one. It seems unbelievable that a player who hit that well should not have won at least one batting championship—but Joe Jackson never did.

Those crazy Pirates

One of the bizarre teams in big league history was the Pittsburgh Pirates in the late 1940s and early '50s. They had two basketball All-Americans playing second base and shortstop (Johnny O'Brien and Eddie O'Brien); a football All-American playing third base (Vic Janowicz); a future top pitcher playing the outfield (Dick Hall); a former outfielder pitching (Johnny Lindell); a left-hander catching (Dale Long); and a symphony orchestra violinist as a utility man (Eddie Basinski). With all that, the Pirates finished last most of those years.

Why "Babe" Ruth?

Babe Ruth spent much of his youth in a home for disadvantaged children in Baltimore. When he was just 18, and still a resident of the home, the Baltimore baseball team signed him. Ruth had never seen much of the outside world, and looked even younger than he really was. When he joined the team, some of the older players spoke of him as a "babe in the woods", and some started calling him "Babe." Sportswriters covering the team picked it up, and the nickname became used so often few people—then or now—know that his real name was George Ruth.

Buhl not a great hitter

What's the big league record for a player coming to bat the most consecutive times without getting a hit? In 1962, Bob Buhl came to bat 70 straight times without a hit.

Advice to ballplayers

Joe McCarthy, who managed the Yankees to eight pennants in the 1930s and '40s, listed these proverbs for anyone who wants to be a good ballplayer. (1) Take your bat off your shoulder, if you want to become a .300 hitter. (2) Outfielders who throw the ball behind the runner lock the barn after the horse is gone. (3) When you start to slide, slide; he who changes his mind may change a good leg for a broken leg. (4) Don't alibi on the bad hops; anybody can stop the good ones. (5) Look ahead, not backwards, on the bases. (6) Don't try to throw the ball before you catch it. (7) Nobody ever became a good ball player by walking after the ball. (8) Don't find too many faults with the umpire; you can't expect him to be as perfect as you are.

Who was Carl Stotz?

The man who started one of the biggest sports ideas ever conceived, is hardly remembered today. Few people recognize the name of Carl Stotz of Williamsport, Pa.—yet he is the man who thought of, and founded Little League baseball. Stotz started Little League baseball in 1939.

Batboy makes more than players

Eddie Bennett was the batboy for the Chicago White Sox in 1919. He told players to rub his shoulder and it would bring them luck. They did, and they won the pennant that year. Bennett got the reputation of being a lucky charm so the Dodgers hired him away in 1920 and THEY won the pennant. By now, just about everybody wanted Bennett, and the Yankees offered him a huge amount of money to come with them for the 1921 season. Bennett did, and the Yanks finished first. By that time, Bennett was making more money than some of the players.

Only one rookie wins batting title

The only rookie to lead a major league in batting at the end of any season was Tony Oliva of the Minnesota Twins, who won the American League batting title in 1964.

Reggie's amazing World Series homers

In the final game of the 1977 World Series, Reggie Jackson hit 3 home runs on the first pitch in 3 consecutive at bats. Thus in his last 3 times up, Jackson had only 3 pitches thrown to him; he took 3 swings, and hit 3 home runs.

What happened to Cooney on Sept. 24 and Sept. 25?

Johnny Cooney played in the big leagues for 23 years, from 1921 to 1944. He hit only 2 home runs in those 23 years, but they came on successive days. He hit one Sept. 24, 1939 and the other Sept. 25, 1939—and he never hit one the previous 18 or the next 5 years.

He never made the majors

One of the most amazing records ever compiled by a baseball player was by Joe Bauman in the Class C Longhorn League in 1954. Bauman not only set the all-time pro baseball record for most homers in one year when he hit 72 that season, but he also batted .400 and drove in 224 runs. Despite that great year in the minors, Bauman never got the chance to come to bat even one time in the big leagues—he never made the majors.

Who's in charge?

Which big league baseball team once played 5 seasons WITHOUT a manager? The Chicago Cubs played from 1961 through 1965 without having a manager. They used a rotating staff of coaches—but no one held the title of manager during those years. They finished in the second division each season.

The two-ball play

A crazy play in big league baseball happened in 1959. Stan Musial was at bat against the Cubs. The pitch was ball four, but it got away from the catcher and rolled to the screen. Musial ran to first, then rounded first and started for second. Alvin Dark, Cub third baseman, ran in to get the ball, picked it up and threw to second. Meanwhile, umpire Vic Delmore had given a new ball to the pitcher. He threw THAT ball to second the same time Dark threw the other ball. One ball sailed into centerfield and, upon seeing that, Musial got up and started to run to third. But shortstop Ernie Banks caught the other ball and tagged Musial out. After much arguing the umps ruled Musial out.

No McGwire or Sosa on this team

The entire Chicago White Sox team of 1908 hit only three home runs ALL SEASON. There have been times in baseball history when ONE player hit three home runs in one game—but here's a whole team that totaled only three homers all year. Despite their lack of power, the White Sox finished 3rd that season with an 88-64 record.

One-legged & one-armed players in big leagues

Two men who overcame disabilities played big league baseball in 1945. Pete Gray who had lost his right arm in a childhood accident played in 77 American League games as an outfielder. When he'd catch the ball in the outfield, he'd throw it into the air, drop his glove, re-catch the ball and throw it to the infield. Bert Shepard, who lost his right leg during World War II, learned to walk and run on an artificial leg and pitched a total of 5 innings also in the American League in 1945.

He hit over .400 for 5 YEARS

In 1921, Hall-of-Famer Rogers Hornsby hit .397; in 1922, .401; in 1923, .384; in 1924, .424; and in 1925, .403. That figures out to a 5-year average of .402. Nobody has ever topped that.

This sounds too good to be true—but it is

In 1962, baseball manager Alvin Dark was watching one of his players, Gaylord Perry, in batting practice. Dark, looking at Perry's lack of power, said, "A man will walk on the moon before Perry hits a home run in the big leagues." Then, 7 years later, on July 20, 1969, Neal Armstrong became the first man to walk on the moon, and—incredibly—on that very day, Perry hit his first major league home run, in a game in San Francisco.

Mother-son combination

There have been more than 100 father-son combinations in major league baseball history—but there was one big league player whose mother played pro baseball. He's Casey Candaele, an infielder who played in the majors in the 1990s. His mother was a star in the All American Girls Pro Baseball League which was featured in the movie, "A League of Their Own." Candaele's mother led the league in batting in 1945.

The shoe polish games

Twice in World Series history, a game was decided by shoe polish—and both times it involved a player named Jones. In the 1957 World Series, Nippy Jones of the Braves claimed he was hit on the foot by a pitch. The umpire first ruled he wasn't—but when the ump was shown the ball had shoe polish on it, he reversed his decision and awarded Jones first base, from where he scored a decisive run. In the 1969 World Series, the same thing happened—this time to Cleon Jones of the Mets. For the second time in a World Series, an umpire reversed his decision after seeing shoe polish on a ball, and again it resulted in a key run.

Only 8 .400 hitters

Of the thousands of men who played major league baseball in the 20th century, only 8 have batted over .400 for a full season. The only 8 to do it were Ty Cobb, Harry Heilmann, Rogers Hornsby, Joe Jackson, Nap Lajoie, George Sisler, Bill Terry and Ted Williams.

Herman triples into a double play

Many experts agree the most bizarre play in big league history happened when Babe Herman of the 1926 Dodgers hit a long drive with the bases loaded. The runner on third scored. The runner on second rounded third but then decided to come back to third. The runner on first ran to third, and Herman, running with his head down, and not realizing the other 2 runners were there, ran full speed and slid into third. All 3 runners were there, and the third baseman, getting the ball, tagged all 3 of them. One was entitled to the base, but the other 2 were out—so Herman achieved immortality by tripling into a double play.

Youngest big leaguer

The youngest person ever to play major league baseball was Joe Nuxhall. He pitched for the Cincinnati Reds in 1944—at age 15.

Alou, Alou and Alou

One of the most unusual lineups in a big league game was San Francisco's one day in 1963. In leftfield was Felipe Alou. In centerfield was Matty Alou. And in rightfield was Jay Alou. That's the only time in major league history that 3 brothers played for the same team at the same time. And not only did the Alous play alongside each other in the outfield, they also batted in succession in the lineup.

Who's in first?

In the Class A Florida State League in midseason 1973, nobody knew who was in first place or what the standings were. The league's record-keeping got confused, and on one day in July, 5 different Florida newspapers carried 5 different sets of standings, and each newspaper had a different team in first place. After a league meeting, they finally got it straightened out.

Best hitter goes zero for 7,000

A baseball player failed to get a hit in over SEVEN-THOUSAND trips to the plate in the big leagues—and yet he was the greatest hitter in history. How's that possible? It happened with Ty Cobb. Cobb holds the highest lifetime batting average in major-league history at .367. He had 11,429 official at bats in his career, and made 4,191 hits for his great .367 average—BUT that means he failed to hit 7,238 times.

Maris' slow start

When Roger Maris broke Babe Ruth's home run record by hitting 61 homers in 1961, Maris had ONLY ONE HOMER THE WHOLE FIRST MONTH OF THAT SEASON. Maris hit only one home run in April that year, then hit 60 homers from May on.

The only Hall of Fame lineup

Fans who went to the 1934 All-Star game saw the only lineup in history where all 9 starters on one team made the Hall of Fame. The starters in that game for the American League were Lou Gehrig, Charlie Gehringer, Joe Cronin and Jimmie Foxx in the infield; Babe Ruth, Heinie Manush and Al Simmons in the outfield; Bill Dickey catching and Lefty Gomez pitching.

Can you name the Big Red Machine?

One of the best teams in baseball history was the Cincinnati "Big Red Machine" of 1975 and '76, which won over 100 games each year and won the World Series both years. Their regular starting lineup was: (1B) Tony Perez; (2B) Joe Morgan; (SS) Dave Concepcion; (3B) Pete Rose; (C) Johnny Bench; (LF) George Foster; (CF) Cesar Geronimo; (RF) Ken Griffey.

Ruth outhomers entire teams

When Babe Ruth hit 60 home runs in 1927, he hit more homers than any other TEAM in the American League that year. The team with the most homers that year, outside of Ruth's Yankees, was the A's who collectively hit 56.

The lonely Browns

In 1935, a big league team, the old St. Louis Browns of the American League, drew only 80,932 fans at home over the ENTIRE season. Today, some big league teams draw more than that on one weekend.

Most grand slams

The all-time record for hitting the most home runs with the bases loaded in history is not held by Babe Ruth or Hank Aaron. The record is held by Lou Gehrig, who hit 23.

Baseball

No team changed managers like this one

A big league team once had 4 different managers in ONE WEEK. It happened to the Texas Rangers in 1977. Frank Lucchesi managed the team until June 22 when Eddie Stanky took over—but Stanky quit after one day. Then coach Connie Ryan managed the team for 3 days until Billy Hunter arrived to manage the team. So the Rangers made baseball history with 4 managers in one week.

The strange career of Paciorek

Of all the men who ever played big league baseball, no one had a career like John Paciorek. He came up to the majors with Houston for the last game of the 1963 season, against the New York Mets. They couldn't get Paciorek out. He got 3 hits in his 3 at bats—but then, NEVER played in a big league game again. A back injury ended his career and he was gone from the majors forever—but he left with a perfect 1.000 batting average.

A dog scores a run in a pro baseball game

In a minor league game in Charlotte, N.C., in 1941, a player hit a long drive to the outfield and started running around the bases. A dog got loose on the field and followed the runner around the bases. Before the fielders could get the ball back to home, the player slid into the plate and was ruled safe by the umpire. The dog followed across the plate before the ball got there—and the umpire gave the safe sign to the dog, too. The official scorer, joining the fun, put the dog's name, and the fact that he scored a run, into the box score.

Best save ever recorded in baseball

Pitchers are credited with saves all the time, but no pitcher ever made a bigger save than pitcher George "Doc" Medich of the Texas Rangers in 1978. Medich was warming up before a game when a fan in the stands suffered a heart attack. Medich had just completed medical school in the off-season and had become a doctor. He ran into the stands, gave emergency treatment, and saved the fan's life.

Fans saw 2 no-hitters in 1 game

Here's the story of one of the most amazing games ever played in big league baseball. On May 2, 1917, pitchers Fred Toney of the Reds and Hippo Vaughn of the Cubs each pitched a no-hitter against each other. At the end of 9 innings neither team had a run or a hit. The Reds finally scored in the 10th to win—but that game stands as the only 9-inning DOUBLE NO-HITTER in major league history.

Woman names baseball

Novelist Jane Austen wrote a book called "Northanger Abbey" in 1816, before baseball was invented. In the book, she said one of the characters liked to play cricket, or base ball. According to the Oxford English Dictionary, that was the first use of the word "baseball."

2 was the fatal number

Did you ever hear the strange story of the "2" jinx about shortstop Ray Chapman, the first man killed in a big league baseball game? Chapman died after being hit by a pitch in a game in 1920. On that day, Chapman batted 2nd in the lineup; he had come to bat 2 official times; he had made 2 hits, each a 2-bagger; he had scored 2 runs; and had stolen 2 bases. In the field he had 2 putouts; made 2 assists and 2 errors. On that fatal day, he had been hit by 2 pitched balls. The 2nd one killed him.

The legendary Satchel

Satchel Paige was so confident of his ability that once while pitching in an exhibition game, he told all his outfielders and infielders to sit down— and then Paige struck out the batter. Another time, with 2 out, he intentionally loaded the bases by walking 3 straight batters so he could face the great slugger Josh Gibson. Paige then struck out Gibson on 3 pitches.

Bizarre error

Rightfielder Larry Walker of Montreal caught a fly ball in a 1994 game. He thought it was the 3rd out of the inning, so he tossed the ball to a fan in the first row. But it was only the second out, and the runner on first base tagged up and started running around the bases after the catch. Walker, finally realizing his mistake, ran back to the fan and pleaded for the ball. He got the ball back and threw it to the infield—but it was too late, and the runner scored.

Hot dogs invented at a baseball game

Harry Stevens was in charge of the concessions at New York baseball games in the early 1900s. One day it was cool and he wasn't selling much cold food. That was all they had at ball parks in those days. During the game he went shopping for something warm he could sell. Stevens bought sausage at a neighborhood butcher shop, and then he added rolls so the fans could hold the sausages—and the hot dog was born. The name "hot dog" was coined by cartoonist Tad Dorgan who was at the game that day and drew a picture of a dachshund in a bun.

Yankees win 14 pennants in 16-year period

The Yankees won the American League pennant in 1949-50-51-52-53-55-56-57-58-60-61-62-63-64. No other major league team has ever come close to that record, before or since.

Who made the most errors?

Oddly enough, the man who was one of the first to be elected to baseball's Hall of Fame, and a man who's been called one of the greatest shortstops of all time, Honus Wagner, made more errors than any big league player in the 20th century. Wagner made 676.

The consistent Mookie

In a baseball statistic that defies odds, major league outfielder Mookie Wilson hit exactly .276 in 1983, .276 in 1984, and .276 in 1985.

3 greats—one position—one city—at the same time

Three members of baseball's Hall of Fame each played the SAME position in the SAME city at the SAME TIME. Willie Mays, Duke Snider and Mickey Mantle each played centerfield for the 3 big league teams in New York City between 1951 and 1957. Mays played for the New York Giants, Snider for the Brooklyn Dodgers and Mantle for the New York Yankees.

Unlucky fan

An incredible coincidence happened in a Philadelphia Phillies game in 1957. Richie Ashburn of the Phils lined a foul ball that hit a fan in the stands. While the fan was being taken up the aisle to the first aid station, Ashburn fouled off the next pitch—which hit the same fan again.

Those holy Reds

The Cincinnati Reds had a pitcher in 1998 named Eddie Priest—which means that over the years the Reds have had on their pitching staffs, a Priest, a Nun (Howie Nunn, 1961-62), a Saint (Randy St. Claire, 1988), and a Church (Bubba Church, 1952-63).

A steady job

One of the most amazing records in sports was set by Connie Mack who managed the same big league baseball team for FIFTY consecutive years. Mack was the manager of the A's from 1901 through 1950. That's a record that will probably never be broken.

He could always hit homers

Here's a true story about Mark McGwire. When he played his first Little League game, at age 10 against a 12-year-old pitcher, McGwire hit a home run over the fence—in his very first at bat.

Baseball

Don't give up on a player too soon

Do you know what kind of start Hall of Famer Willie Mays had when he first came to the big leagues? The first 12 times he went to bat he failed to hit. Then he got a hit his 13th time up—but then went to bat 14 more consecutive times without a hit. Thus, in his first 27 times up in the majors, he had just one hit, and his batting average was .037. At that moment few people would have said that Willie Mays would become one of the greatest players of all time.

23-year-old big league manager

Who was the youngest man ever to manage a big league team? The answer is Roger Peckinpaugh, who was only 23 when he was picked as manager of the Yankees in 1914. Lou Boudreau is the second-youngest manager in major league history. Boudreau was only 24 when he was named manager of the Indians in 1942.

He struck out sitting on bench

In a 1952 game, Sammy White of the Boston Red Sox had 2 strikes on him and was replaced by a pinch-hitter. The pinch-hitter took a third strike—but under baseball scoring rules, the strikeout was charged to White since he had 2 of the 3 strikes. White struck out while sitting in the dugout.

Hoyt started like a McGwire, but didn't finish that way

There was a baseball player who hit a home run on his first at bat in the big leagues—but, then he played for 20 years and never hit another. Hoyt Wilhelm hit a home run his first time up in the majors in 1952. His major league career lasted until 1972; he appeared in over 1,000 games; but never hit another homer.

If you're a lefty, try baseball

Only about 15% of the U.S. population is left-handed, yet surprisingly, almost 30% of major league baseball players are left-handed.

He never hit one over the fence, but led in homers

A man led a major league in home runs one season—yet never hit one ball out of the park or over the fence all year. He was Tommy Leach who played for the Pittsburgh Pirates in 1902. Leach led the National League in homers that year—but every one of his home runs was an inside-the-park homer. He never hit one over the fence—yet he wound up being the home run champion.

They didn't sell this one out

Ever wonder what was the smallest crowd ever to see a major league baseball game? The record low was set in 1890 in a National League game in Pittsburgh. Official paid attendance at that game—6.

A baseball riddle

How can you throw a baseball with all your might and have it stop, and come right back to you, WITHOUT IT HITTING A WALL, OR A BAT, OR ANY OTHER KIND OF OBJECT? Surprisingly few people can come up with the answer. A ball will stop, and come back to you, if you throw it straight up in the air.

Who wants a .400 hitter?

You'd think having a .400 hitter would help a team, but no major league team ever won a pennant when one of their regular players hit over .400. Since 1900, there have been 13 times when a big leaguer hit over .400 for the season—and on each of those 13 occasions, the team with a .400 hitter failed to finish first. Any manager would welcome a .400 hitter, yet so far, all of them have been jinxes as far as winning a pennant is concerned.

Manager turns down World Series

In 1904, the Giants won the National League pennant but their manager, John McGraw, refused to let them play the American League winner, the Red Sox. McGraw at that time hated the American League. He thought the league should never have been formed. He had such power in baseball then, that no World Series was played in 1904.

Who played in the most World Series games?

Yankee catcher Yogi Berra set the record by playing in 75 World Series games.

Troy in big leagues

The smallest city ever to have a big league baseball team was Troy, N.Y. Troy was in the National League from 1879 to 1882.

Fly ball never came down

It happened at the indoor Minneapolis Metrodome on May 4, 1984. Dave Kingman of Oakland hit a high fly ball that got caught in the netting of the fabric ceiling of the dome. The ball stuck there and didn't come down. The umpires decided it was a ground rule double.

Batter refuses hit

In 1942 when Hall-of-Famer Paul Waner hit a grounder that went off the shortstop's glove, Waner got to first base, and the official scorer called it a hit. But Waner at that time had 2,999 hits and he wanted his 3,000th hit to be a clean one—so he waved to the press box asking the hit to be changed to an error. The scorer complied, and that hit was taken away from Waner. That's probably the only time any baseball batter ever refused a hit.

Cubs win!

What are the most runs ever scored by one team in one big league game? The record is 36, by the Cubs in 1897. They won that game 36-7.

Baseball puzzler

How can a batter have 10 pitches thrown to him during one time at bat—with none of them being fouls—and still remain at bat? The batter comes up with two out and a runner on first base, and gets a count of 3 and 2. Then the runner at first is out stealing, ending that inning. The same batter would lead off the next inning with what officially is still considered the same time at bat, and again runs the count to 3 and 2, thus giving him 10 pitches, with no fouls, in one time at bat.

Maybe they had a pitching problem

One of the strangest teams in big league history was the 1930 Phillies. All eight regular players on that team batted over .300 that year—yet the team finished in LAST place.

So close

This is the unusual story of a man who came WITHIN SECONDS of fulfilling a dream of playing in a big league baseball game—but then had the chance taken away. In 1971, pitcher Larry Yount was called from the bullpen by Houston to pitch in his first game. While warming up, on the mound, he injured his arm, marking the end of his major league career, in which he never threw an official pitch.

Ted Williams had guts

Here's the story about how Williams became the last man to hit .400 in a major league season. It happened in 1941 when he went into the last two games of the year hitting an even .400. Those last two games were meaningless as far as the pennant race went, and Williams could have sat out the games to insure himself batting .400. But he wanted to play. Williams, with all the pressure, got an amazing six hits in his last eight at bats, and would up batting .406 for the season.

The 6-inch home run

In a minor league game some years ago, a batter hit the ball a few inches in front of the plate. The umpire called it fair, but the pitcher and catcher thought the ball hit off the batter's foot before rolling in front of the plate, which would have made it foul. They stood and argued with the ump, the ball resting 6 inches from home, while the batter raced around the bases and crossed the plate—with what turned out to be the shortest home run of all time.

Why "southpaws'?

Ever wonder why left-hand pitchers in baseball are called "southpaws." Ball parks are usually laid out so the batter faces east to avoid a setting sun shining in his eyes. So, if centerfield is east, the south end of ball parks parallels the first base line. A left-hand pitcher's throwing hand is on the first base side of the diamond. Thus, he's a "southpaw."

It would be tough to beat Cy Young's record

The record for most games won by a pitcher in big league history was set by Cy Young, who won 511 games in his career. To appreciate how hard it is to win 511 games, consider this: It's difficult for any pitcher to win 20 games in any one year; few pitchers ever win 20 games in three or four or five different seasons; but to win 511 games, as Cy Young did, you'd have to average 20 wins a year, every year, for over 25 years.

This team was bad

Big league baseball has never seen another team like Cleveland in 1899. That year, Cleveland set the all-time record by finishing 80 games out of first place. Of the 154 games they played, they lost 134 of them while winning only 20 all year—another all-time record. Their 2 top pitchers won a grand total of 4 games each.

Why couldn't these managers go on the field?

There were 2 big league managers in 1950 who were NOT allowed to go out on the field to change pitchers or argue with the umpires. They were the manager of the Dodgers, Burt Shotton, and the manager of the A's, Connie Mack. The reason they couldn't go on the field? They always managed in street clothes, and not uniforms. Baseball rules prohibit anyone from going on the field during a game unless they're in uniform. Shotton and Mack were the last big league managers to manage in street clothes.

Yanks, Dodgers, Giants set amazing World Series record

For 18 years in a row, from 1949 through 1966, EVERY World Series featured either the Yankees, Dodgers or Giants. One of those teams was in every World Series during all those years.

The Mother's Day oddity

Here's a famous sports story about Mother's Day with a strange coincidence. On Mother's Day, 1939, future Hall of Fame pitcher Bob Feller brought his mother to Chicago so she could see him pitch for the first time in the big leagues. In the game, Feller threw a pitch and the batter fouled it off, hitting a spectator in the stands. Of all the thousands of people there, who did that foul ball hit? Ironically, on Mother's Day, it hit Feller's mother. Feller raced over to the stands, made sure his mother was okay after some quick first aid—and then returned to the mound and struck out the batter.

What's chess got to do with baseball?

Why is a first-year player in baseball called a "rookie"? The name came from chess, where the rook is often the last piece played. In the early days of baseball, first-year players were usually the last used. They became known as "rooks" or "rookies."

He still made the Hall of Fame

What player struck out in his only time at bat in the majors—and fumbled half of all the fielding chances he ever had—yet is now in baseball's Hall of Fame? Answer is Walter Alston. Alston played in only one big league game in his career, for the Cardinals in 1936, and struck out his one time up. He also made one error in the 2 career fielding chances he had. But he became a successful manager, leading the Dodgers to 7 pennants between 1955 and 1974. He was elected to the Hall of Fame for his managerial record in 1983.

First place wasn't good enough

A big league manager was fired when his team was in first place—because his bosses thought he should be farther ahead than he was. The Philadelphia Phillies fired manager Pat Corrales on July 18, 1983 with the Phils in first place, one game ahead of second place.

The perfect ballplayer

There was a major league player who had a lifetime batting average of 1.000, a lifetime fielding average of 1.000 AND a lifetime pitching record of 1.000. The man who made this amazing record was John Kull. He pitched for the A's in 1909 and played only one big league game in his life—but in that one game, he was the winning pitcher, he went one-for-one at bat, and had one chance in the field which he handled without error. He never played again but he became unique in baseball history. He's the only man ever to retire with a perfect big league record in batting, fielding and pitching.

Top this, McGwire and Sosa

There was once a big league player who hit a home run EVERY time he got a hit one season. He was Clem Labine, a Dodger pitcher. In 1955, Labine made only 3 hits all season—but every one of those hits was a homer.

The zany "Eddies Game"

In a game in 1948, Eddie Stevens was playing first base for the Pirates, Eddie Bockman was playing third, and Eddie Fitzgerald was catching. The batter hit a pop fly near the mound. Eddie Stevens came over from first, Eddie Bockman came over from third and Eddie Fitzgerald came out from the plate toward the ball. The pitcher, forgetting all 3 players had the same first name, shouted, "Eddie, you take it." All three Eddies, looking up at the ball, crashed into each other. The ball fell to the ground for a base hit.

Home Run Baker?

The big league baseball player whose famous nickname was "Home Run" Baker never hit many homers. Baker played in the majors from 1908 to 1921 and got his nickname because he once hit two homers in a World Series—and the name stuck even though he never hit many home runs before or after that.

Why bullpen?

Why is the bullpen in baseball called a bullpen? It started in the early 1900s when many ballparks had advertising signs down the left and right field lines for Bull Durham tobacco, displaying a big picture of a bull. That's the area where relief pitchers warmed up, and those areas began to be called "bullpens."

He didn't go out to the ball game

Jack Norworth, who wrote the most famous baseball song of all time, "Take Me Out To The Ball Game," had never seen a baseball game when he wrote that song—and what's even stranger is this: after he wrote the song in 1906, and became famous and made lots of money from it, Norworth waited 34 more years—until 1940—to go see his first big league game.

Last to first in a month

Believe it or not, there was a big league team that was in last place as late as Aug. 30 one year—and yet they won the pennant. The New York Mets were in last place Aug. 30, 1973—but despite that, incredibly, they won the pennant that season.

Baseball is a funny game

Announcer Ernie Harwell made a list of strange oddities about baseball: The right-handed batter's box is on the same side of the field as left field. The word strike, which means to hit an object, is used when a batter misses a pitch or doesn't swing at all. A batted ball hitting the foul line is a fair ball. And spring training starts in winter.

Three

Basketball

He lost at his own game

The inventor of basketball, James Naismith, was a LOSING coach in the sport he originated. After inventing basketball, Naismith became head basketball coach at the University of Kansas for 9 seasons, but his overall record was only 53 wins and 56 losses.

Michael Jordan cut?

Surprisingly, Michael Jordan did NOT make the varsity team when he tried out for basketball as a sophomore in high school, in Wilmington, N.C. Arguably the best player in history was cut. But he did make the team in his junior year—and went on to his great college and pro career.

Basketball

Those girls could win

What are the most games in a row any
basketball team ever won? The most amazing streak
by any team in high school, college or pro ball was
the one by the Baskin (La.) High School girls' team.
Between 1947 and 1953, they won—not just 100
straight games or 150 straight or 200 straight—but
the unbelievable total of 218 consecutive games to
set the all time record.

Referee was the coach

For the NBA season of 1954-55, the Pistons
picked a referee to be their new head coach. They
selected NBA referee Charley Eckman as their head
coach even though he had never been a coach
anywhere before that—and, the amazing thing is, the
Pistons finished in first place that season.

The basketball player who couldn't beat fate

In 1977, David Furr tried out for the University of Evansville basketball team but he injured an ankle and was dropped from the team. He then became the team's statistician for home games only. On Dec. 14, all members of the Evansville team were killed in a plane crash on the way to a road game. Furr wasn't on that plane and you'd say he was lucky to have injured his ankle, and lucky again that the university didn't take him to away games as a statistician. But right after the team's plane crashed, Furr was driving his car near Evansville. The car skidded on a patch of ice, collided with a truck and Furr was killed instantly. It seemed that David Furr's time was up whether he made that fatal air trip with the Evansville basketball team or not.

A game with no fouls

In 1972, in a game in Maryland, between Rockville and Paint Branch high schools, Rockville won 60-44, and, not one foul was called during the entire game. The game took only 57 minutes with no foul shots.

Basketball

It was both the highest-scoring game— and the lowest scoring

Boone County High of Kentucky beat Newport High 117-111 in 1984 to set the record for the highest-scoring game in Kentucky high school history. But it was later discovered that a Boone player was ineligible. Boone had to forfeit the game, and that changed the official score to 1-0, making it the lowest-scoring game in state high school history.

Overtime after overtime

The longest basketball game in either high school, college or pro history, was played by 2 North Carolina high schools when Mamers High defeated Angier High in a game that went through 13 overtime periods.

Owner fired team, kept coach

Usually it works the other way, but when Ned Doyle owned Miami of the American Basketball Association, his team had a bad year in 1969-70, so he got all new players for the next season, but kept his coach, Hal Blitman. That's probably the only time that's happened in professional sports history.

What a final

One of the strangest basketball games of all time was the one played for the championship of the 1936 Olympics. In those days, they played basketball outdoors on dirt in the Olympics, and on the day of the finals, there was a heavy rainstorm. Not only did the players play in the rain, but the court was a quagmire with everyone slipping and sliding, covered with mud, and hardly able to dribble. The U.S. won, beating Canada, 19-8, but that game goes down in history as the most unusual world championship basketball game ever played.

119

The player who revolutionized basketball

Before Hank Luisetti came along, basketball players took their shots with two hands. But Luisetti, who played for Stanford in the 1936-37 season, revolutionized the game by shooting the ball with one hand. He set scoring records that season, getting as many as the then-unheard-of-total of 50 points in one game. Even with Luisetti's success, most coaches didn't want their players to use the one-hand shot— but soon players started experimenting with it, and the one-hand style swept the nation and changed basketball forever. Luisetti's one-hand shot made for faster play and·more scoring because players didn't have to stop and set themselves for a two-hand shot, as before.

Durable Wilt

Wilt Chamberlain played EVERY MINUTE of 79 NBA games in the 1961-62 season—NEVER coming out for a substitute. That's an all-time NBA record for durability for that many games.

A believe-it-or-not game

A basketball team once scored only one point in an entire game—and yet won the game. It happened on March 7, 1930 when Georgetown High of Illinois beat Homer High, 1-0. The only scoring in the game was one foul shot by Georgetown.

The shortest game

In Nampa, Idaho in 1979, a crowd of about 1,000 people plus bands and cheerleaders turned out for a basketball game that lasted exactly ONE SECOND. The night before, a high school game had ended in a dispute over whether the clock was started properly in the last second of the game. The next day, officials ruled that the last second had to be replayed. So, players, spectators, bands and cheerleaders came back for that one-second replay. Even a radio station broadcast it. It had to be the shortest event in sports history.

Team refuses to play for national title

Marquette was chosen to play in the NCAA tournament in 1970—but they rejected the invitation. Coach Al McGuire was unhappy with the regional section in which his team was placed, so he turned down the NCAA and gave up any chance to win the national championship that year.

Lakers misnamed

One of the strangest team nicknames in sports is the Los Angeles Lakers of the NBA. The franchise started in 1947 in Minneapolis, Minnesota. Minnesota is known as "The Land of 10,000 Lakes," so the team was called the Minneapolis Lakers. In 1959, the team was moved to Los Angeles, and they kept the nickname of Lakers—even though Los Angeles is certainly NOT famous for lakes.

Unbelievable comeback

The greatest comeback by a team in a college basketball game happened on Jan. 6, 1990. Butte Community College of Oroville, Calif. was behind 17 points with just 77 seconds to go against Shasta College. Many fans left, assuming Shasta was a big winner. But Butte rallied to win the game. Incredibly, they scored 18 points on a combination of field goals, and personal and technical fouls in just 77 seconds.

That incredible Tar Heel team

One of the most amazing college basketball teams of all time was the North Carolina Tar Heels in 1956-57. They never lost a game all season, and in the NCAA tournament they won the semi-final in triple overtime—then, the next night won the championship game ALSO in triple overtime, beating the Wilt Chamberlain-led Kansas team. North Carolina was led by All-American Lennie Rosenbluth.

3-player team better than 5

An unusual game in college basketball was played March 7, 1968 when Duquesne beat St. Francis 85-74. What made this game amazing is because many of their players fouled out, Duquesne was left with only 3 players on the floor against 5 for St. Francis in the last 2 minutes, 23 seconds—and Duquesne not only held on to win, but actually increased their lead.

Winning was in the blood

The greatest record ever made by a basketball coach was by a high school coach, Ernest Blood. Blood coached at Potsdam (N.Y.) High School for 9 years from 1906 to 1915 and NEVER LOST A GAME. Then he moved to Passaic (N.J.) High School where he lost just once. In the first 201 games he coached, his record was 200 victories and one loss. Blood was elected to the basketball Hall of Fame in 1960.

They missed them all

Has any college basketball team ever missed EVERY shot from the field they tried in a game? In 1938, Adrian College missed all their field goal attempts in a game against Albion. They set the NCAA record for the fewest field goals in a game (zero) while losing 76-4, scoring on just 4 foul shots.

Homeless team wins title

A team once won the national championship in college basketball even though they never played a home game that season. Holy Cross was the 1947 national champion but they had no gym or arena of their own that year. They played every game on the road. Yet they were able to win 27 of 30 games, including 23 in a row, and won the college basketball championship of the nation.

Who was drafted ahead of Jordan?

Surprisingly, Michael Jordan was NOT drafted first when he came into the National Basketball Association in 1984. Two players were picked ahead of Jordan—Hakeem Olajuwon and Sam Bowie.

Literally no-names

A college basketball team once had a school nickname of "No-Names." Siena College of Loudonville, N.Y., dropped its former name, "Indians," in 1988—and while they were deciding on a new name, they played the entire 1988-89 season WITHOUT a name. The media that year called them the Siena "NoNames." For the 1989-90 season they chose "Saints," which is still their nickname.

The winner is?

There was a college basketball game when the result was changed TWICE, AFTER the game was over. West Virginia scored at the buzzer to beat St. Joseph's by one point in a game in 1985. West Virginia celebrated the victory. But 7 minutes later, officials decided the last shot came too late, and they gave the win to St. Joseph's. But, 2 days later, the conference commissioner overruled the officials and gave the victory back to West Virginia.

New meaning for a road game

A high school basketball team once literally played a home game on the road. In 1952, Charlotte High School of Punta Gorda, Fla., scheduled one of its home games outside on a road. They installed portable baskets and painted markings on a street in their town, and set up bleachers along the sidewalks.

Basketball

7,000 losses

A basketball coach lost over SEVEN THOUSAND CONSECUTIVE GAMES—to the same team—and he wasn't fired. He's Red Klotz who coached the Washington Generals. The Generals played the Harlem Globetrotters in each game—and the Globetrotters beat Klotz's Generals over 7,000 straight times.

You know those NBA players are tall

If the 348 players in the National Basketball Association were stacked one on top of each other, they would reach more than 1,000 FEET HIGHER THAN THE EMPIRE STATE BUILDING. The Empire State Building is 1,414 feet high, and the combined height of the stacked NBA players would be over 2,400 feet.

The prolific Lisa

In a girls high school game in 1990, Lisa Leslie of Morningside High in Inglewood, Calif., scored 101 points IN ONE HALF. That record has never been topped. Leslie didn't score any more points because the other team forfeited the game at halftime. Leslie went on to become a star at Southern Cal, and in pro basketball.

They didn't lose in Los Angeles

Oddly, the longest winning streaks in the history of college basketball AND in the NBA were both achieved by 2 teams from the same city in the same years. The longest college winning streak ever was 88 straight victories by UCLA from 1970 to 1974. The longest NBA winning streak in history was 33 straight by the Los Angeles Lakers in 1971-72.

Shouldn't basketball be in Winter Olympics?

We all know regular basketball seasons are played in the winter months—so why do the Olympics put basketball in the Summer Olympics? There's a rule that says all sports in the Winter Olympics must be contested on ice or snow and, therefore, that makes basketball a Summer Olympic sport.

Players looked down on president

The National Basketball Association has for years featured some of the tallest athletes in the world—yet the man who helped organize the league and was its president for many years, Maurice Podoloff, stood only 5-3.

Trick basketball question

Name the only school who won the NCAA tournament in men's basketball and is NOT located in any of the 50 states. The answer: Georgetown, which won the NCAA basketball tournament in 1984. Georgetown is in the District of Columbia.

He scored them all

Has any basketball player ever scored all his team's points in a high-scoring game? This amazing feat happened in a high school game in Alabama. A player named Walter Garrett scored 97 points in one game and the final score in that game was 97-54.

Miss America's son

Kiki Vandeweghe, who played many years in the NBA, is the son of Coleen Hutchins Vandeweghe. Coleen was Miss America in 1952. Her husband, Ernie, also played in the NBA, as did her brother, Mel Hutchins.

Another one of Wilt's amazing records

Did you know that Wilt Chamberlain, who played in over 1,000 NBA games in his career, NEVER fouled out of a game in his 14 seasons in the league?

Best foul shooter never played

The greatest foul shooter in basketball history never played basketball. Bunny Levitt once made 499 consecutive foul shots for the all-time record. In the 1930s, touring with the Harlem Globetrotters, a cash prize of $1,000 was offered to anyone who could beat him in a contest of 100 foul shots. No one ever did. The best of any challenger was 86, and Bunny's worst was 96. But, Levitt never played in a basketball game. He was only 5-4 and contented himself with holding foul-shooting exhibitions.

School enters NCAA tourney with one name—and leaves with another

Texas Western entered the NCAA tournament in 1967 playing its first game on March 11, and won, advancing to the next round. But before they played the next game, on March 17, the name of the school was changed to University of Texas at El Paso, or UTEP. And so, they started the tournament as Texas Western, and left it as UTEP.

Celtics stand alone

The Boston Celtics of the NBA are the only team in the history of major professional sports to win a league championship 8 years in a row. Closest any other pro team has ever come are the Montreal Canadiens in hockey who won the Stanley Cup 5 straight years and the New York Yankees in baseball who won 5 consecutive World Series. The Celtics won the NBA title 8 straight years from 1959 through 1966.

Who was Luther Gulick?

There's one name hardly any basketball fan has ever heard of—yet if it had not been for this man, the game of basketball might not be here today. In 1891, Luther H. Gulick asked James Naismith to develop a game that could be played indoors in the winter. Gulick was head of the physical education department at Springfield College where Naismith was an instructor. Naismith then invented basketball—but if Gulick never gave Naismith the suggestion to invent an indoor game, it might not have been done. Gulick also originated the YMCA logo.

Kareem a winner

When Kareem Abdul-Jabbar played high school and college basketball, the teams he played on had 187 wins and only 3 losses. In high school in New York, his team won 78 and lost 1. In college at UCLA, his freshman team had a record of 21-0, and in 3 years of varsity ball, he was on the winning side 88 times and the losing side only twice.

This record may never be broken

An incredible record was set by UCLA—and to realize how incredible it was, consider this. Today, it's unusual for any college basketball team to win the NCAA tournament even 2 years in a row, but UCLA won it an amazing SEVEN years in a row— EVERY year from 1967 through 1973.

The fabulous Carr Creek boys

One of the legendary basketball teams of all time was the Carr Creek (Ky.) high school team of 1928. There were just 8 boys on the squad—all related to each other. They were from a small mountain community and played in homemade uniforms on a homemade court. But they amazed everyone—and captured national attention—by reaching the state finals where they finally lost in 4 overtimes.

200 points in a game

Has any college basketball team ever scored 200 points in one game? The first team to do that was Troy State of Alabama which beat DeVry of Georgia on Jan. 12, 1992 by the score of 258 to 141. Troy State made 51 3-point baskets.

They weren't invited—but they still won

A team that was NOT invited to the NCAA basketball tournament WON the tournament that year. Utah was left out of the 1944 NCAA tourney— but at the last minute, they were called on to replace the Arkansas team that was in an automobile accident. And then—Utah went on to win the championship.

Poor Naismith

The man who invented basketball, James Naismith, never got one penny for his invention even though basketball takes in millions of dollars every year.

Basketball could have been boxball

If it wasn't for a janitor, basketball might well be called "boxball" today. Originally, James Naismith wanted to use square boxes—and not round baskets—as the goals when he invented the game. He asked a janitor to nail square boxes at each end of the gym. But the janitor couldn't find square boxes, so he selected two round half-bushel peach baskets—by chance—and the players started calling the game "basketball" instead of perhaps calling it "boxball."

Four

Golf

Why golf courses have 18 holes

In the early days of golf's development in Scotland, different courses had different numbers of holes. For example, when the first British Open was played, at the Prestwick Club in 1860, that course had only 12 holes. Some other courses then had 7 holes, some had 8, some had 14. But the most famous course, St. Andrews of Scotland, just happened to have 18 holes—and in the years following 1860, other courses increased to 18 holes merely to follow the pattern set by St. Andrews. Thus 18 holes became the standard for golf courses everywhere.

A new way to finish in the money

At the Western Open in 1939, Oscar Grimes hit a shot that bounced into a snack bar just off the fairway. The ball hit a key on the cash register, bounced up and then dropped right into the opened money drawer.

The ultimate hole-in-one frustration

One of the strangest shots in golf happened when Bob Rosburg made a HOLE-IN-ONE THAT WASN'T A HOLE-IN-ONE. Rosburg hit a drive off the 12th tee but the ball hooked badly, hit a tree and bounced crazily the wrong way—not to the 12th green—but to the 13th and right into the cup. It was the rarest of golf shots—a hole-in-one in the wrong hole.

What score does average golfer shoot?

According to a survey by the National Golf Foundation, the average non-pro golfer shoots about 97 for 18 holes. They say only one-third of all golfers regularly break 90, and only 8 percent shoot in the 70s.

Bobby the Master

How great a golfer was Bobby Jones? In the years from 1923 until he retired in 1930, Jones played in 21 major tournaments including the U.S. Open, British Open, U.S. Amateur and British Amateur—and in those 21 tournaments, Jones finished first or second in all but four. No other golfer in history has ever come close to that percentage of success.

The reason golf courses have sand traps

The oldest golf courses in the world—in Scotland—are situated by the sea. Sandy spots are on the courses by nature. So when other courses were built elsewhere, sand traps were added to make the courses more like the original ones in Scotland.

Those dimpled golf balls

Why are there indentations, or dimples, on a golf ball? Golf balls, being so small, would be more easily driven off course by wind if it weren't for the indentations that tend to keep the ball straighter in flight.

A one-in-a-million shot

While pro golfer Tony Jacklin was playing in a tournament, he hit a 300-yard-long shot that landed right in a spectator's pocket—without any injury to the spectator.

Miracle hole-in-one

The longest hole-in-one anyone ever made was by Robert Mittera, on the 10th hole of the Miracle Hill Golf Course in Omaha, Neb., on Oct. 7, 1965. He made a hole-in-one of 444 yards.

That's a big golf course

A man once hit golf balls clear across the United States, from California to New York. Floyd Rood, in 1963, walked across the country hitting golf balls as he went. He used over 3,000 golf balls and took over 114, 000 shots.

Why "birdie"?

Why is the word "birdie" used in golf to describe a hole that is made in one shot less than par? In the 1800s, "birdie" was a popular slang expression for "good." Golfers would say, "I made a birdie of a shot." The word "birdie" became a recognized part of golf when anyone played better than par.

He didn't even stop for a sandwich

One of the strangest things in golf occurred at a course in England in 1974. Nigel Denham hit his approach shot to the 18th green, but the ball bounced out of bounds and landed in the clubhouse restaurant. He went into the restaurant and shot the ball back through the window right onto the green.

An Open oddity

It was at the 1989 U.S. Open. Experts say the odds were more than a million to one. What happened were 4 holes-in-one in the same tournament, on the same hole, on the same day. On June 16, 1989 at the Oak Hill Country Club in Rochester, N.Y., Doug Weaver made a hole-in-one on the 167-yard, par-3 6th hole. Then Mark Wiebe did it. Then Jerry Pate did it. Then Nick Price did it. Each player used a 7-iron.

Byron Nelson's unbeatable streak

One of the most incredible records in golf was set by Byron Nelson when he finished first in ELEVEN tournaments IN A ROW on the PGA Tour in 1945. To realize how amazing that record is, consider this: It's unusual today for any pro golfer to finish first in even 2 or 3 consecutive tournaments— so Nelson's record may last forever.

He used his head the wrong way

A bizarre event happened in the 1934 U.S. Open when Bobby Cruickshank was battling for the lead. He hit a good shot and was so happy, he threw his club in the air. But the club came down and hit him on the head, almost knocking him out. He wobbled through the rest of the round unable to play well—and lost his chance to win.

The oldest golf course in the U.S.?

The first golf course built in the U.S. is the Foxburg Golf Club, Foxburg, Pa., some 60 miles northeast of Pittsburgh. It opened in 1887 and is still in existence. Second-oldest is St. Andrews in Yonkers, N.Y., established in 1888.

What a start

On Aug. 17, 1996, a 9-year-old-girl, Randi Wilson, in Seaforth, Ont., made a hole-in-one on the first swing on the first shot she ever made on a golf course. She made it on a 103-yard hole. According to the Associated Press, there's no record of anybody ever doing that before.

One-hour putt

There's one golf course in the world where it takes a putt over one hour to travel 6 feet. The course is on the border between Finland and Sweden and the border runs right through the 6th green. Because Sweden is one time zone west of Finland, a successful 6-foot putt that leaves your putter at 1 p.m. in Sweden drops into the cup shortly after 2 p.m. in Finland.

He took only one club

One of the most unusual golf rounds in history was played by Emmett French. In 1921, he played a Pinehurst, N.C., course entirely with a putter—using no other club—and despite that, French was able to score an 80.

3 holes-in-one

In an unbelievable feat in 1962, an amateur golfer, Dr. Joseph Boydstone of Bakersfield, Calif., scored three holes-in-one during ONE 9-hole round on a regulation course.

The amazing Ben Hogan

In 1949, Ben Hogan's legs, hips and pelvis were badly injured in an auto accident, and doctors doubted he'd ever walk again, let alone play competitive golf. But Hogan didn't give up. To the surprise of everyone, he entered the 1950 U.S. Open. Playing in pain, and with bandages over much of his body, he outplayed the greatest golfers in the world and won the Open that year, and the next year.

The great Jones never finished among money-winners

Here's an amazing fact in these days of high-paid sports stars. Bobby Jones, one of the greatest golfers of all time, who won the U.S. Open 4 times and the British Open 3 times, never won any money in golf. Despite being a world-class player, playing with all the great pro golfers of his time, Jones remained an amateur throughout his career and never accepted money for winning a golf tournament in his life.

What a hole

Any golfer who thinks they've had a bad round should feel better after reading this. A golfer at the Shawnee Invitational in 1912 had a score of 166 on ONE hole in that tournament. It happened when the golfer's tee shot went into a lake, and later into a woods, and with one thing leading to another, this unfortunate golfer would up with 166 strokes on that hole. That's believed to be the worst score ever made for one hole in any organized golf tournament.

Back-to-back holes-in-one

Incredibly, a golfer once made holes-in-one on 2 CONSECUTIVE par-4 holes. On Sept. 2, 1964, Norman Manley accomplished that feat on the seventh and eighth holes at the Del Valle Country Club in Saugus, Calif.

Snead's famous jinx

All-time great golfer Sam Snead could never win the U.S Open—and his jinx began when he had the 1939 Open almost wrapped up. But he just missed winning it when his putt on the final hole rimmed the cup and spun out. Snead played in the Open 40 more years and—despite winning every other major tournament on the golf tour—he never did win the U.S Open.

Top golfer dies on golf course

An ironic twist occurred in the death of champion golfer, Tony Lema. In July, 1966, Lema was flying from Akron, Ohio to Chicago when his plane crashed, of all places, on a golf course. Lema was killed on the 7th hole of a course near Lansing, Ill.

Take this, slow golfers

What's the fastest anyone ever played 18 holes of golf? The world record was set by Len Richardson who once played a 6,248-yard, 18-hole course, holing out on each hole, in 31 minutes. Richardson was an Olympic runner and ran at top speed between each shot.

Who says holes-in-one are difficult to make?

Although holes-in-one are thought to be something special, American golfers average about 40,000 HOLES-IN-ONE EVERY YEAR. That's according to a golf clearinghouse which keeps track of them. Sports Illustrated reports that the number of holes-in-one since 1952 have ranged from about 38,000 to 42,000 per year.

No tee

During the first few hundred years of golf, no one played the game with a golf tee. The golf tee wasn't invented until 1920. And it wasn't invented by a golf pro, but by a New Jersey dentist, Dr. William Lowell. Before Dr. Lowell invented golf tees, golfers teed-up their shots with mounds of dirt.

Youngest to make hole-in-one

According to official records, a 6-year-old boy became the youngest person to make a hole-in-one on a regulation course. It was made by 6-year-old Tommy Moore on the 145-yard 4th hole at Woodbrier Golf Course in Martinsburg, W. Va., on March 8, 1968. And to make his record even more amazing, Tommy also made another hole-in-one before he turned 7.

The incredible Montague

One of the most amazing golfers of all time was a little known man named John Montague who, during the 1930s, developed some of the most fantastic feats ever seen on a golf course. He was able to hit moving targets with a golf shot—and one time he shot an 80 over 18 holes using a shovel, rake and baseball bat instead of conventional golf clubs. Playing seriously, he once shot a 58 at a Palm Springs club, bettering the course record by 7 strokes. He was probably the greatest shot control artist in the history of the game, but is hardly remembered today.

Another sign that times have changed

When Paul Runyan was the top golf money winner in the U.S. in 1934, he won a total of $6,767 all year—and after deducting his travel and caddie fees, his net for the year was $11.98. And he was the leading money winner on the golf tour that year.

Why is golf called golf?

Although golf was developed in Scotland, it was the Dutch who gave the game its name. The word "golf" is a Dutch word meaning a club with which to hit a ball.

Five

Auto Racing...Boxing

Putting fast in perspective

When auto race drivers go as fast as 200 miles-per-hour, as some do in qualifying for races, that's equivalent to driving THE LENGTH OF A FOOTBALL FIELD IN JUST OVER ONE SECOND. A car traveling 200 miles-per-hour is going 275 feet a second, and a football field is 100 yards, or 300 feet long, so a car at that speed would go from goal line to goal line in just over one second.

Double knock out

There was a world championship boxing match in which BOTH fighters KNOCKED EACH OTHER OUT at the SAME TIME. In a 1912 lightweight title fight, Joe Rivers and Ad Wolgast each swung and KO'd each other. Both fell to the floor. The referee ruled Rivers was the loser because he hit the floor a split second before Wolgast. Therefore, he said, Rivers was counted out first, and Wolgast, although also knocked out, was the winner.

Why Indy?

Why did the Indianapolis 500-mile auto race get started in Indianapolis—and not some other city? The Indianapolis track was built in 1909 when the city of Indianapolis was a center of the auto industry with many auto manufacturers located there. Early auto people wanted a proving ground for their nearby factories, and so the track was built in Indianapolis.

Incredible fight

In Paris, France, on April 17, 1909 Sam McVey met Joe Jeannette. Jeannette was knocked down 49 times in that fight—but despite being knocked down all those times, Jeannette—amazingly—won the fight. McVey was so tired, he failed to answer the bell for the last round.

No pit stop

Did anyone ever complete all 500 miles of the Indianapolis 500-mile auto race WITHOUT making a pit stop? In 1931 Clessie Cummins entered a diesel-powered car and he finished the 500 miles with NO stops to make history, even though he finished in 13th place.

Upside-down win

One of the unusual auto races of all time was the 1952 Florida Stock Car championship. A car was in first place near the end of the race when its wheels came off. The car flipped over—but crossed the finish line first, skidding on its top across the line.

Talk about a long fight

A pro boxing bout once lasted an incredible 7 hours and 19 minutes. Imagine 2 fighters slugging it out that long. It happened when there was no limit on rounds. In 1893 Andy Bowen and Jack Burke fought 110 rounds in New Orleans. That's the longest fight in boxing history.

Winner does NOT drive across finish line

One of the strangest big-time auto races ever was the Indy-500 of 1915. The winner of that race, Ralph DePalma, won by pushing his car—by hand—across the finish line. DePalma was leading the field when his car broke down a few yards from the finish. He got out and pushed it the rest of the way—and he won the Indy-500.

KO almost preceded fight

In 1936, two top boxers of the day, Tony Canzoneri and Jimmy McLarnin were to meet in a bout. They came to the center of the ring before the fight, but Canzoneri was hit on his head by the ring microphone that had been lowered for the introductions. He was almost knocked out and the fight was almost over before it started. But he recovered – and went on to win the fight.

Why the Indy-500 is 500 miles

When the Indianapolis 500-mile auto race was first held in 1911, its founder, Carl Fischer, wanted a long endurance race that would still give spectators time to get in and out all in daylight. With top racing speeds in those days of around 75 mph, 500 miles was chosen as the most practical long distance—and tradition has kept it at 500 miles ever since.

He KO'd himself

A boxer knocked himself out in a bout in 1992. In the New York Golden Gloves competition, a boxer was warming up in his corner before his fight. While shadow boxing, he accidentally punched himself in the face, causing a bloody nose. Doctors wouldn't allow him to fight. He had to forfeit his match—knocking himself out of the bout.

Who held heavyweight title the longest?

The record is held by Joe Louis. Louis was the heavyweight champ for an incredible 11 years and 8 months, from 1937 to 1949.

The shape of boxing

Why is a boxing ring called a "ring" when, in fact, it's a square? In the early days of boxing, fighters fought in a circular area and the word "ring" remained even though the shape of the fighting area changed.

Brothers are champs

What 2 brothers both won the heavyweight boxing championship of the world? They are Leon Spinks, who was heavyweight champ in 1978 and his brother, Michael, who won the heavyweight championship in 1985.

Fastest car

What's the fastest a car has ever gone on land? The record was set in 1997 when a jet-powered car went 764 mph on Nevada's Black Rock Desert—going faster than the speed of sound.

Johnson vs. Johnson for title

There was a boxing bout for the heavyweight championship of the world in which both fighters had the same last name—and neither fighter won. In 1913, heavyweight champion Jack Johnson fought challenger Jim Johnson. The fight ended in a draw.

He won heavyweight title while on the canvas

Max Schmeling won the heavyweight championship of the world while on his back. In 1930, Jack Sharkey knocked Schmeling down in the 4th round of their title fight, but the punch was called a foul blow. Because of the foul, Sharkey was disqualified and the championship was awarded to Schmeling—as he was lying on his back.

That's a skid

The longest skid marks ever made by a car were by Craig Breedlove's jet-powered car after it went out of control at the Bonneville Salt Flats in 1964. The skid marks were nearly 6 miles long.

He didn't hold title very long

The shortest time any boxer ever held a world championship was 3 HOURS. Young Stribling was declared a winner of a fight for the world light-heavyweight championship on Oct. 4, 1923. But 3 hours later, officials reversed their decision and took the fight—and the title—away from Stribling.

No punches in this fight

It happened in a bout in 1943 at Bristol, England between Louis Fetters and Carmine Milone. At the bell starting the first round, Milone rushed toward Fetters so fast that he lost his balance, fell, struck his head on the ring post, was knocked unconscious and counted out by the referee.

Those old speed demons

How fast could you drive a car in the old days? The first auto race in the United States was held in Chicago on Thanksgiving Day, 1895. It was a 50-mile race, and the winning car, driven by famous inventor Frank Duryea, traveled at the average speed of—7 ½ miles per hour.

Longest auto race

There was a special duration auto race in Paris in 1933 that lasted 133 days, from March to July. At the end of the race, the drivers had covered over 185,000 miles.

The fighters weren't KO'D—but the ref was

In a 1948 bout, the referee stepped between welterweights Mike DeCosmo and Larry Buxton while they were swinging away. Both fighters simultaneously and accidentally hit the ref and knocked him out. The fighters were left standing while the referee was lying on the canvas.

Six

Hockey...Soccer...Tennis

Nothing could stop Lemieux

During the 1992-93 season, Mario Lemieux had to sit out 24 games in midseason because of Hodgkin's disease. But he returned—and despite his illness, plus 22 physically-draining radiation treatments, and the missed games, HE STILL LED the National Hockey League in scoring for that season.

Why is it soccer?

Ever wonder why soccer is called soccer? In England, soccer was called "Association Football" because it was governed by the London Football Association. That was often shortened in newspapers to "Assoc. Football" and gradually, "Assoc." was changed to ""soccer."

Will the real Chris Evert stand up

How's this possible? In sports in 1974, Chris Evert won the Wimbledon tennis tournament and Chris Evert was ALSO voted the top 3-year-old horse of the year. This oddity happened when Chris Evert, the tennis player, won Wimbledon in 1974—and meanwhile, there was a race horse named Chris Evert in 1974, and Chris Evert, the horse, was voted the best 3-year-old filly of the year.

Why love?

Why is the score of zero in tennis called "love"? It came from the French word "l'oeuf" which means egg, as in goose egg or zero. In the early days of tennis, when the game was more genteel, it was thought bad form to tell an opponent he or she had a zero or nothing score, so "love" was adopted to make it sound better.

Most goals by one team, one game

The Montreal Canadiens set the NHL record when they scored 16 goals in a game in 1920. No NHL team has equaled that in all the years since.

The one-name player

The person generally considered the greatest soccer player in history is Pelé, who used only that name by itself. He was born in Brazil in 1940, and his real name was Edson Arantes do Nascimento. As Pelé, he led Brazil to 3 World Cup titles. And he later played for the New York Cosmos of the North American Soccer League.

He never hit a backhand

There was a tennis champion who would switch his racket from one hand to another so he always hit a forehand shot. Georgio de Stefani, who won the French championship in the 1930s, NEVER had to hit a backhand shot because of his ability to hit the ball holding the racket with either his right or left hand.

He might have had a headache

In setting the world soccer record of ball control, Huh Nam Jim of South Korea juggled a soccer ball with his head, feet and legs—but not his hands—for 17 hours nonstop, without the ball ever touching the ground. It happened at an exhibition in 1991.

The incredible Helen Wills

Helen Wills NEVER LOST A MATCH, AND NEVER LOST EVEN A SET during 5 YEARS of play in major tournaments all over the world. Wills compiled that amazing streak between 1927 and 1932—and that's a feat that's never been duplicated in world-class tennis.

The amazing Mr. Davidson

Gary Davidson founded the World Hockey Association in the 1970s and signed many NHL stars, creating havoc within the NHL. But when he founded the league, Davidson had never seen a hockey game in his life.

Longest match in history

In a doubles match in 1968, Mark Cox and Bob Wilson defeated Charlie Pasarell and Rom Holmberg at Salisbury, Md.—before tie-breakers were used—by the scores of 26-24, 17-19, 30-28. The match took six hours and 23 minutes to set the all-time official record.

Who's the woman whose name is on the Stanley Cup?

When the Detroit Red Wings won the Stanley Cup in 1952, '54 and '55, the president of the team was the daughter of Red Wings founder, James Norris. As president, Marguerite Norris Riker, got her name on the Stanley Cup.

Stanley never saw Stanley Cup game

The man who donated the Stanley Cup to hockey, Lord Stanley, never saw a Stanley Cup hockey game in his life. Lord Stanley was the governor-general of Canada, but never went to the playoff games named for him.

Hockey's unusual periods

Ever wonder why ice hockey games are played in 3 periods with 2 intermissions, while other sports like football, basketball and soccer have just one intermission or halftime? The reason is that 2 intermissions are needed in hockey games to repair the ice and make it playable.

A change of name

When tennis started, it had a different name. Tennis was invented by British Maj. Walter Wingfield and he called it "sphairistike" after a similar game played in India. Later the name was changed to "lawn tennis," and finally, simply, tennis.

Tennis Hall-of-Famer flunks tennis

One of the greatest tennis players of all time, Bill Tilden, who was the top player in the world in the 1920s, was unable to make his college tennis team. Tilden went to the University of Pennsylvania and failed to make the tennis team. A few years later he won every major tennis tournament in the world.

167

Soccer balls started another sport

In 1891, when the game of basketball was invented, no basketballs had yet been designed. So, James Naismith, who invented basketball, used available soccer balls instead. Soccer balls continued to be used in the early years of basketball. Thus, the first basketballs were soccer balls.

Why CHC for Montreal

One of the most famous uniform designs in sports is worn by the Montreal Canadiens who have "CHC" on the front of their jerseys—but most people don't know what that CHC stands for...it's Club de Hockey Canadien. Montreal has been wearing that same uniform design since 1917.

They don't dress like teammates

In which sport does one player have to wear a different-color uniform than the rest of his or her teammates? Answer is soccer where the goalie must wear a different uniform.

Tennis' unusual scoring

Why are points in tennis called 15, 30, and 40, instead of 1, 2, and 3? In the early days of tennis, the score was kept on a clock with the hands moved to 15, 30 and 45 minutes after the hour, so the points were called 15, 30, and 45. Later, players changed the 45 to 40, but the 15 and 30 remain.

Regular season doesn't count much

Incredibly, a LOSING team once won the championship of a major pro sports league. In the 1937-38 season, the Chicago Black Hawks of the NHL won only 14 of 48 games during the regular season, but they qualified for the playoffs—and then surprisingly knocked off each team they met in the post season to win the Stanley Cup.

Goalie was red hot—the wrong way

One of the strangest things in hockey happened in a 1930 game when the puck was shot at goalie Albie Goldberry. The puck struck a pack of matches he had put in his pocket. The impact of the puck hitting the matches set fire to Goldberry's uniform. Goldberry received burns before teammates could put out the fire.

Loser is winner

An oddity of tennis is that you can lose more games than your opponent in a match—yet still win that match. A tennis score of 0-6, 7-5, 7-5, for example, would mean the winning player won 14 games while the losing player won 16. But even though a player lost 16-14 in games, that player would have won the match.

Nepotism in the NHL

What pro sports team was coached by a son-father-grandfather combination? It's the New York Rangers of the NHL. Craig Patrick coached the Rangers in 1984-85. His father, Lynn, coached the Rangers from 1948 to 1950, and his grandfather, Lester, coached the Rangers from 1926 to 1939.

Bad grammar in the NHL

One of sport's most famous teams has a nickname that is grammatically wrong. It is the Toronto Maple Leafs of the NHL. The usual plural of "leaf" is "leaves"—not "leafs"—so they should really be the Toronto "Maple Leaves" instead of the "Maple Leafs."

Sometimes it doesn't pay to celebrate

In 1993, Steve Morrow scored the winning goal to give his team the English Cup soccer championship. His teammates gathered around him and tossed him in the air in celebration. Unfortunately, they failed to catch him. Later, as his teammates were accepting the trophy, Morrow was being helped off the field with a broken arm.

Seven

Miscellaneous

Low score is best

Can you name 2 sports in which the low score—and NOT the high score—wins? Answer is golf and cross-country running.

The unusual Olympic record

Who's the only athlete to win gold medals in BOTH the Summer and Winter Olympics? This unique achievement was accomplished by Eddie Eagan. He won a gold medal in the Summer Olympics in boxing in 1920, and a gold medal in the Winter Olympics in the bobsled in 1932.

Why the Kentucky Derby is called a derby

In 1780 a British sportsman, the Earl of Derby, founded a famous horse race in Epsom, England which was named in his honor and called Derby's Race at Epsom or the Epsom Derby. When officials in Kentucky began their race in 1875, they borrowed the English name and called it "The Kentucky Derby."

Worse than a shutout

There was a team that not only didn't score any points in a contest, but actually wound up with a MINUS score. It happened to Loyola College of Baltimore in 1978 in a dual wrestling meet. Loyola lost all 10 of its matches against the University of Maryland AND was also penalized a point for arguing with the referee—so the final score was Maryland 51, and Loyola MINUS 1.

Do you think ticket prices are high today?

What's the highest price ever charged for a ticket to one sports event in America? Would you believe $100,000? That all-time record was set Aug. 4, 1944, during World War II, when a fight was staged to sell U.S. war bonds. It was a light-heavyweight championship bout between Beau Jack and Bob Montgomery. To get a ringside seat for that fight, you had to buy a $100,000 war bond.

The strangest Kentucky Derby

Nobody knew who won the 1968 Derby FOR TWO YEARS. Although Dancer's Image finished first, it was found he had been given a pain-killing drug, and he was temporarily disqualified. There were court suits and counter-suits. Finally, it was ruled that the second-place horse, Forward Pass, was the official winner. But that ruling didn't come until 1970—two years after that Derby had been run.

Is it in or out?

Oddly, there are some sports in which the ball is in-bounds when it hits the sideline—and there are other sports in which the ball is out-of-bounds when it hits that line. The ball is "in" when it hits the line in baseball and tennis—and it's "out" when it hits the line in basketball and football.

What an athlete

One person in sports history did ALL these things. He played for 6 different National Football League teams. He played for 3 different big league baseball teams. He won 2 gold medals in the Olympics. He served as first president of the league that became the NFL. He was also a track star. The person who did all that was Jim Thorpe—voted the best athlete of the first half of the 20th century in the AP poll.

Two Halls of Fame

Who's the only person in history to be elected to BOTH the pro football Hall of Fame AND the big league baseball Hall of Fame? The only person to achieve that is Cal Hubbard. He was a great NFL lineman in the 1920s and '30s. He was voted into pro football's Hall of Fame in 1963. After his football career, Hubbard became a top umpire in big league baseball and was voted into baseball's Hall of Fame in 1976.

Fastest fastball

In what sport does the ball travel faster than in any other? Answer is jai-alai where the ball can travel over 180 mph.

Mother-son in Olympics

A mother-son combination once participated in the Olympics for the United States. The only mother-son combination ever to do that was Alice Arden Hodge who competed in track and field in the 1936 Olympics, and her son, Russ Hodge, who took part in the decathlon in the 1964 Olympics.

Great nickname

One of the best nicknames for any sports team is the one used by Poca High School in Poca, W. Va. They name their teams the Poca Dots.

Walking coast-to-coast in 9 hours

John Deni, who set many Olympic records in his career, once walked from the Atlantic Ocean to the Pacific Ocean in 9 hours. He did it in the Panama Canal Zone where the distance from the Atlantic to the Pacific is short enough to make such a feat possible.

Lying down on the job

A horse once won a race while lying down. In a 1931 race, a horse named Brampton tripped and fell. He rolled over and was lying on the ground with his nose over the finish line and his jockey still hanging on. This happened before the number two horse crossed the finish line, so Brampton was declared the winner even though he was lying on the ground.

Heisman winners play big league baseball

In the history of baseball and football, Bo Jackson and Vic Janowicz were the only athletes to play in major league baseball after winning the Heisman Trophy in football. Janowicz won the Heisman at Ohio State in 1950 and played big league baseball in 1953 and 1954. Jackson won the Heisman at Auburn in 1985 and started his big league baseball career in 1986.

Why badminton is called badminton

Badminton was first played at the estate of the Duke of Beaufort in England and the Duke's estate was named "Badminton." The sport took its name from the Duke's home.

Try this quiz

In which sports are the playing fields or areas the following lengths? (A) from 3-4 miles; (B) 78 feet; (C) 9 feet; (D) 62 feet 10 1/8 inches? The answers: (A) golf; (B) tennis; (C) table tennis; (D) bowling.

Going Backward

Can you name the three sports in which the winners cross the finish line going backward? They are rowing, tug-of-war, and the backstroke in swimming.

The amazing Bob Mathias

The Olympic decathlon is composed of 10 events including pole vaulting and javelin throwing. It was won in the 1948 Olympics by Bob Mathias of the U.S.—even though Mathias had NEVER IN HIS LIFE pole vaulted or thrown a javelin until that year. Despite complete inexperience in the pole vault and javelin, Mathias was able to beat the other great athletes of the world in the decathlon—and he set a world record doing it.

Youngest Olympic winners

A 12-year old boy once won a gold medal at the Olympics. Bernard Malivoire of France won a gold medal in the 1952 Olympics by serving as the coxswain in a rowing event. Youngest girl to win an Olympic gold medal was 13-year-old Marjorie Gestring of the U.S. who won a swimming event in the 1936 Games.

The strangest horse race

In Australia in 1903, three horses, High Flyer, Loch Lochie and Bardini finished in a triple tie for first. Then they re-ran the race and they finished in a triple tie for first again. The odds are enormous against any triple dead heat, but for that to happen twice in a row defies any odds.

Manager vs. coach

Why is the person in charge of a team on a baseball field called a "manager"—while in every other sport the person in charge on the field is called a "coach"? It goes back to the beginnings of baseball when the person in charge took care of off-field duties as well, such as booking games, arranging transportation and running the front office. So he was called a "manager." In football and other sports, such jobs were usually split and the person who led the players on the field came to be called a "coach."

Neves rose from the dead

One of the most incredible sports stories of all time concerns the famous jockey, Ralph Neves. He won many races for 26 years AFTER he was pronounced dead. Neves was thrown from a horse in a race at Bay Meadows in 1936 and was trampled by another horse after the spill. Medical men on the scene pronounced Neves dead—but a half-hour later, he not only regained consciousness, but was riding again the next day, and he went on to win over 3,000 races during the next 26 years.

Why are skating jumps called axels, salchows and lutzes?

Each is derived from the name of the skater who invented or popularized them. The axel stems from Axel Paulsen of Norway. The salchow jump is named for Ulrich Salchow of Sweden. The lutz is named after Alois Lutz of Switzerland.

Talk about long-distance runners

There was once a man who ran across the United States TWICE. In 1928, Harry Abrams ran from Los Angeles to New York, a distance of 3,422 miles, in 84 days. Then in 1929, he ran from New York back to Los Angeles. He averaged about 41 miles per day.

They didn't play the national anthem

If you had been able to go to a football or baseball game or some other sports event in any year up to the 1930s, you would NOT have heard the public address announcer say before the game, "Here's our national anthem," followed by the playing of *The Star Spangled Banner*. Congress didn't make *The Star Spangled Banner* the national anthem until 1931. And even then, few teams played it. It wasn't until World War II in the 1940s that teams began playing it as a patriotic gesture and started the tradition that continues today.

Winners can't repeat

In which major sport are champions prevented from defending their title? In horse racing, in certain races like the Kentucky Derby, Preakness and Belmont Stakes, only horses of a certain age can take part, and the winning horse can't come back the next year because they're one year older.

Sure bet

A race horse was once virtually assured of winning a race BEFORE it was run. For the 1948 Pimlico Special, 20 horses were entered, but one of those horses was the great Citation. When the other owners found out that Citation was definitely going to run, they withdrew one by one, figuring they had no chance to win, so great was his record then. Only one horse—Citation—went to the post that day. He ran the race all by himself and chalked up the easiest win in his successful career.

Miscellaneous

They really started something

When was the first time a sports event was ever on TV? It was on May 17, 1939 when an experimental station in New York City made history by televising a college baseball game between Princeton and Columbia. The announcer was Bill Stern.

Why it's important to get an education

How tough is it to become a player on a major professional sports team? According to a recent report, only one of every 12,500 high school basketball players will make it to the NBA. Only one of every 4,000 high school baseball players will someday play in the big leagues. And only one in 5,000 high school football players will play in the NFL.

Ms. Samuelson goes extra 2 miles

One of the greatest athletic feats was performed by runner Joan Benoit Samuelson. She was on her way to run in the Boston Marathon in 1979 when she got caught in traffic. She got out of the car and ran 2 miles to the starting line. Then she immediately ran the marathon—and not only won it, but did it in record time.

Husband-wife combination in Hall of Fame

The only husband-and-wife combination who are both in a major sports Hall of Fame are the late Don Drysdale who's in the baseball Hall of Fame for his pitching with the Dodgers, and his wife, Ann Meyers who's in the basketball Hall of Fame. She was an All-America at UCLA.

The dress code has changed

Until the 1940s, most male golfers usually played wearing a tie, and male tennis players wore long sleeve shirts and long pants on the courts.

Who was first player to have number retired?

When Lou Gehrig left baseball in 1939 because of the disease which has since been named after him, his number 4 was retired by the New York Yankees—and that started the tradition of retiring numbers.

Greatest track performance

One man broke 3 different world track records all in one afternoon—all within an hour-and-a-half. This was done by Jesse Owens of Ohio State at an Ohio State-Michigan track meet, May 25, 1935. He broke the world record for the 100-yard dash, the 220-yard dash and the long jump in a period of 90 minutes. And if that wasn't enough, he also tied the world record for the 220-yard low hurdles that same afternoon.

Super Bowl & World Series

Can you name the only athlete who's played in BOTH the World Series AND the Super Bowl? The only person who's done that is Deion Sanders. Sanders played in the World Series with the Braves, and the Super Bowl with the 49ers and Cowboys.

What does ESPN stand for?

Although sports fans always hear the name ESPN—the cable-TV sports network—few know what the letters ESPN stand for. It's Entertainment and Sports Programming Network. ESPN began in 1979.

This sport is #1

What's the #1 participation sport in the U.S.? According to a recent report, 52 million people bowl—making bowling #1. More than 20% of the U.S. population bowled last year.

The Winner didn't win

When did The Winner NOT finish first, second or third in the Kentucky Derby? It happened in the 1896 Derby. There was a horse in that race whose name was The Winner. But The Winner didn't win—and finished far back in the field.

A true upset

Here's one of the most amazing oddities in sports. A horse whose name happened to be Upset pulled off the greatest upset in horse racing history. He upset the great Man O' War on Aug. 13, 1919. That was the only race Man O' War ever lost—and he lost to Upset.

The unusual name of skiing

Ever wonder why skiing is called skiing? The work "ski" is a Norwegian word for "snowshoe."

Winning was really important here

No athletes ever had pressure to win like the pancration athletes in the ancient Olympics. The pancration was a 2-man fight combining boxing and wrestling—and was held until a contestant was killed. The winner won an Olympic medal, but the loser lost his life.

One athlete—7 medals

Of all the athletes who've ever competed in the Olympics, which one set the record for winning the most gold medals in any one Olympics? The all-time record is held by U.S. swimmer Mark Spitz. Spitz won 7 gold medals at the 1972 Olympics, and nobody has ever topped that.

This may surprise you

Which distance is greater—running once around the bases in baseball, or running the full length of a football field from goal line to goal line? Answer is the trip around the bases. It's 90 feet between each base, so a trip around the bases is 360 feet, or 120 yards, while the distance from goal line to goal line on a football field is just 100 yards.

One of the classic trivia questions

One man—amazingly—was BOTH the head coach of a National Football League team AND the manager of a major league baseball team in his career. Who was he? Answer: Hugo Bezdek who was head coach of Cleveland in the NFL in 1937-38, and manager of Pittsburgh in big league baseball in 1917 through 1919.